ESSAYS IN PAN-AMERICANISM

Essays in
Pan-Americanism

By
JOSEPH BYRNE LOCKEY

◆

KENNIKAT PRESS, INC./PORT WASHINGTON, N. Y.

ESSAY IN PAN-AMERICANISM

Copyright 1939 by the Regents of the University of California
Reissued in 1967 by Kennikat Press by arrangement

Library of Congress Catalog Card No: 66-25927
Manufactured in the United States of America

Analyzed in the ESSAY & GENERAL LITERATURE INDEX

Preface

THE PAPERS included in this volume have all been printed before. Two of them, the first and the last in the series, appeared in the *American Journal of International Law*. Two others formed a part of the sketch of James G. Blaine which the author contributed to a work edited by Samuel Flagg Bemis and published by Alfred A. Knopf under the title of *The American Secretaries of State and their Diplomacy*. Of the rest, one was published in *The Hispanic American Historical Review*, one in *The American Historical Review*, one in the *Quarterly* of the Florida Historical Society, one in *The Pacific Historical Review*, and finally, one in the *Boletín* of the Venezuelan Academy of History. For permission to reprint these scattered bits in the present form, the author is under obligations to the various publishers concerned.

The subject of inter-American unity, upon which all the papers bear with more or less directness, is of timely interest. In a world torn by dissension, it is heartening to find the twenty-one republics of this continent living in peace and striving to perfect a system for the maintenance of peace among themselves. If this little volume contributes in some degree to the understanding of so important a development in the relations between the states of the New World, its purpose will be served.

J. B. L.

June 1, 1939

Contents

	PAGE
The Meaning of Pan-Americanism	1

Reprinted, with slight revision, from the *American Journal of International Law*, Vol. XIX, No. 1, January, 1925

Diplomatic Futility 23

Reprinted from the *Hispanic American Historical Review*, Vol. X, No. 3, August, 1930

The Pan-Americanism of Blaine 51

Reprinted, with slight modifications, from *The American Secretaries of State and their Diplomacy*, Vol. VII, pp. 272–287, and Vol. VIII, pp. 155–163

Blaine and the First Conference 71

Reprinted from *The American Secretaries of State and their Diplomacy*, Vol. VIII, pp. 164–181

An Aspect of Isthmian Diplomacy 85

Reprinted from the *American Historical Review*, Vol. XLI, No. 2, January, 1936

Toledo's Florida Intrigues 97

Reprinted from the *Florida Historical Society Quarterly*, Vol. XII, No. 4, April, 1934

Shaler's Pan-American Scheme 125

Reprinted from the *Pacific Historical Review*, Vol. II, No. 4, December, 1933

Bolívar after a Century 135

Read before the American Historical Association, December 29, 1930, and published in the *Boletín de la Academia Nacional de la Historia* (Venezuela), Tomo XIV, No. 53

Pan-Americanism and Imperialism 143

Delivered in substantially its present form as the presidential address before the Pacific Coast Branch of the American Historical Association, December 29, 1937, and published in the *American Journal of International Law*, Vol. XXXII, No. 2, April, 1938

The Meaning of Pan-Americanism

WHAT IS Pan-Americanism? The term itself is new. It appears to have been employed first by the New York *Evening Post*[1] in discussions relating to the International American Conference which was held at Washington in 1889–1890. It was used in imitation doubtless of such terms as Pan-Slavism, Pan-Hellenism, and Pan-Islamism, which, along with numerous combinations of the sort, became current during the third quarter of the last century. The new term was quickly admitted into the columns of other newspapers, and, as in the course of a few years its use became general, it found its way into the editions of the dictionaries and encyclopedias which subsequently appeared. To such works of reference inquirers who have but a vague notion of its meaning are most likely to turn for their first instruction on the subject. Unfortunately, however, from this source but little enlightenment is to be obtained.

A careful comparison of the definitions of the standard dictionaries and encyclopedias reveals but one point upon which they are wholly in accord: they all agree in limiting the scope of Pan-Americanism to the independent states of the New World. In spite of the etymology of the word we may regard this point as settled. Pan-Americanism has to do with the sovereign states of the continent and not with the continent as a whole. On one other point the definitions approach agreement, in that they all either assert or imply a union of states; but we are left in doubt as to the character of the union. In one case it is described as an alliance. As understood in public law an alliance is a defensive, or defensive and offensive, league between states and the parties are bound by treaties. There are no Pan-American treaties of alliance, and, it is safe to assert, there is no Pan-American alliance. Hence the elimination of

---
[1] Superior figures refer to notes on page 163.

this term from the description of Pan-Americanism is to be desired. In another case the term federation is employed. But a federation is a union of states in which the separate parts lose their identity in international intercourse. A federation, and likewise a confederation, is an international person. The separate states of the United States constitute a federation, but the independent states of the Western Hemisphere do not, for they have not surrendered their sovereignty or any part of it to any Pan-American authority. Accordingly this term also should be eliminated. Finally, though we accept the general idea of union, we are uncertain whether it is political or non-political in character. The answer to this important question must await the further development of our analysis.

Some inquiry must now be made regarding the position of the United States in this union of New World republics, for on this point there is much confusion of thought. One of the definitions, that of *La Grande Encyclopédie,* declares that Pan-Americanism tends to group the American republics under the hegemony of the United States. This may mean much or little, depending on the definition of hegemony. The term has certain definite historical associations. Athens, for example, exercised hegemony in the Delian League; but that league was not of equal states and Athens stood in the relation of sovereign to some members of the group. Sparta in the Peloponnesian Confederation is another example. In this case, it is true, the league appears to have been composed of equal states. But the leadership of Sparta was military in its nature. It was exercised for the purpose of waging war more effectively on other states. Still another example is provided by the German Confederation of 1815, in which Prussia is said to have exercised hegemony. In this case Prussia was a preponderant power in a society of states which had entered into a covenant establishing a supreme authority over all, an authority which Prussia was destined to usurp. Which of these conceptions of hegemony, if any, is applicable to the position of the United States

The Meaning of Pan-Americanism

in the Western Hemisphere? Surely no one uses the term in the Spartan or military sense, and to apply it as it was applied to Athens or to Prussia would seem in effect to deny the principle of state equality, with all the implications of such a denial. This is a vital point and requires a word of consideration. Much has been written on the subject of state equality, and though publicists from the time of Grotius have generally supported the principle, yet occasionally a voice is raised in denial of it. Lorimer, for example, says that it is a chimera as unrealizable as the union of the head of a woman and the tail of a fish. The statesmen, jurists, and publicists of the United States, however, have invariably adhered to the doctrine. Jefferson proclaimed it in unmistakable terms in the opening sentence of the Declaration of Independence when he spoke of the united colonies assuming among the powers of the earth the separate and equal station to which the Laws of Nature and of Nature's God entitled them.

Chief Justice Marshall championed the doctrine less dramatically but no less forcibly when he said: "No principle of general law is more universally acknowledged, than the perfect equality of nations."[2] And Elihu Root in a memorable address before the delegates of the Third International American Conference, assembled at Rio de Janeiro, in 1906, declared:

> We deem the independence and equal rights of the smallest and weakest member of the family of nations entitled to as much respect as those of the greatest empire; and we deem the observance of that respect the chief guaranty of the weak against the oppression of the strong. We neither claim nor desire any rights or privileges or powers that we do not freely concede to every American republic. We wish to increase our prosperity, to expand our trade, to grow in wealth, in wisdom and in spirit; but our conception of the true way to accomplish this is not to pull down others and profit by their ruin, but to help all friends to a common prosperity and a common growth, that we may all become greater and stronger together.[3]

It must be remembered that the equality of which we are speaking is legal equality, equality before international law.

Most publicists contend that state equality does not extend beyond the sphere of legal rights. They generally maintain that from the political point of view the states of the world are not all equal. Westlake, one of the profoundest of the later writers on international law, says: "A state may be so weak that it is not much or at all consulted by the other powers, and that little attention is paid to its opinion, if given. In that case," he adds, "it is in a position of political inferiority, and many states of the European system are permanently in such a situation toward what are called the great powers, yet their equality is not necessarily infringed thereby."[4] Thus Westlake reaches the conclusion that a certain sort of political inequality is compatible in the European system with legal equality. He omits any direct reference to the American state system, but Lawrence, an able contemporary, makes good the omission. He points out the disparity in strength and influence between the United States and any other power in the Western Hemisphere, and he accords to this republic because of its preponderant strength and influence a position in America similar to that occupied in Europe by the Great Powers. But he is careful to point out differences, the most important of which is that the United States is not called upon in the exercise of what he calls its primacy to dictate territorial arrangements with a view to maintaining a shifting balance of power.[5] This difference is so fundamental, and the preponderant influence of the United States is exercised in a manner so different from the way in which the concert of Europe is made effective, that the comparison between the two systems is hardly valid. The marks of contrast are rather more striking.

It is worthy of observation that no one authorized to speak for the United States has ever made any claims which can fairly be said to infringe either the political or the legal equality of the independent states of America. The term hegemony has never been admitted into our official vocabulary, though such words as superiority, priority, and supremacy have occasion-

The Meaning of Pan-Americanism

ally crept into the state papers emanating from Washington. But the use of these terms has always been accompanied by explanations which left the user under no suspicion of denying equality. An example may be cited in the language which Secretary of State Fish employed in a report to President Grant in 1870. He said:

The United States by the priority of their independence, by the stability of their institutions, by the regard of their people for the forms of law, by their resources as a government, by their naval power, by their commercial enterprise, by the attractions which they offer to European immigration, by the prodigious internal development of their resources and wealth, and by the intellectual life of their population, occupy of necessity a prominent position on this continent which they neither can nor should abdicate, which entitles them to a leading voice, and which imposes on them duties of right and honor regarding American questions, whether those questions affect emancipated colonies, or colonies still subject to European dominion.[6]

The special position of the United States was later so emphatically reaffirmed by the Cleveland administration in connection with the Anglo-Venezuelan boundary dispute as to subject the government to the charge of ignoring the principle of equality. It is true that Secretary of State Olney in his instructions to Thomas F. Bayard, the American ambassador at London, declared: "Today the United States is practically sovereign on this continent, and its fiat is law upon subjects to which it confines its interposition." Standing alone, the statement is doubtless susceptible to an imperialistic interpretation, and many critics both at home and abroad preferred to wrench it from its context and give it such an interpretation. These critics were unfair to Olney, for he went on to ground his remarkable declaration on the infinite resources of the United States, which, "combined with its isolated position, render it master of the situation and practically invulnerable as against any or all other powers. All the advantages of this superiority," he said, "are at once imperiled if the principle be admitted that European powers may convert American states into colonies or provinces of their own."

Moreover, Olney expressly disclaimed any intention on the part of the United States to interfere in the internal affairs of the other American republics. "The Monroe Doctrine," he declared, "does not establish any general protectorate by the United States over the other American States. . . . The rule in question has but a single purpose and object. It is that no European power or combination of powers shall forcibly deprive an American state of the right and power of self-government and of shaping for itself its own political fortunes and destinies." This is an assertion, not a denial, of equality. Some observers contend that the practice of the United States has not always conformed to its professions. In support of their contention they point to armed interventions in Cuba, the Dominican Republic, Haiti, and Nicaragua; and they raise the question whether Cuba under the Platt Amendment could have enjoyed, or the other republics under their special treaty arrangements with the United States can enjoy, perfect equality.

It is well established in international law that the occasional obedience of one state to the commands, or even its habitual submission to the influence, of other states does not impair its sovereignty.[8] It follows that if the sovereignty of such a state is not impaired, its equality is not infringed. Whether the restrictions placed upon Cuba by the Platt Amendment were sufficient to reduce it to an inferior status is a question upon which publicists do not agree.[9] But as Cuba was accepted in the society of nations as fully sovereign it would have been illogical—it would be even more so now that the offending Amendment has been abrogated[10]—to deny its equality. The same reasoning applies to the other states mentioned. It was never the purpose of the United States to exercise permanent dominion over any of them. The interventions, ill advised as they now seem to have been, came to an end leaving behind a deposit of treaty restrictions; but these restrictions do not

The Meaning of Pan-Americanism

seem to derogate from the sovereignty of the states concerned nor to infringe their equality before international law.

This digression on the subject of equality has been made for the purpose of inquiring into the validity of the assertion that Pan-Americanism implies a union of American states under the hegemony of the United States. The term hegemony would not be objectionable if it meant no more than leadership derived from preponderant power and influence, without impairment of equality. But since there remains always a doubt as to what is meant by hegemony, and since the term has no exact meaning in public law, it should be avoided in a description of Pan-Americanism. As has already been indicated, American statesmen do not employ it, and, it may be added, the later practice of the State Department seems to eschew such terms as superiority, priority, and supremacy. The national existence of weak states rests on the principle of equality. Realizing this, they are jealous of its strict observance. They are quick to detect and to cry out against any tendency to ignore it, and they are no less quick to recognize and to applaud any movement to give it greater force. The weaker American states have become particularly concerned about its maintenance, for events of the past generation have filled some of them with doubts and forebodings. The United States, traditionally a champion of equality, should in the course of time convince the world of its genuine attachment to the principle. Failure to do so would leave Pan-Americanism under the suspicion of being a mask for imperialism.

Thus far in our quest of the meaning of Pan-Americanism we have arrived at agreement on but two or three points. The conception, we have seen, embraces the independent states of America and it involves their union, as we have attempted to demonstrate, on a basis of equality. The set definitions can be of no more service to us. In the hope of finding a more adequate conception set forth in the public declarations of the leading American statesmen, let us now turn to them for further enlightenment. We should expect to find in their expressions on occasions of the International American Conferences, if at any time, the views which they hold on the subject of inter-American relations. The first of these conferences was convened at Washington in 1889. At that time James G. Blaine was secretary of state. He had for several years been an ardent advocate of Pan-American solidarity. As secretary of state in Garfield's administration, eight years before, he had taken steps to convene the American republics at Washington; but owing to Garfield's death and the subsequent resignation of Blaine from the Arthur cabinet, the plan was abandoned. However, Blaine did not give up the idea of bringing representatives of the American nations together at Washington, and when it finally fell to his lot to preside over their counsels he brought to his task the matured thought of an able statesman as well as the consummate skill of a brilliant diplomat.

As secretary of state, Blaine welcomed the delegates to this first International American Conference, and he took advantage of the occasion to set forth what may be termed his Pan-American creed. So admirably concise in form and so lofty in conception was his address that it deserves to rank among the greatest pronouncements of American statesmen. No summary of such an address could possibly do justice to its power and effectiveness. And yet we must attempt it.

Conscious of our common fate as inhabitants of the New World, Blaine declared that like situations beget like sympathies and impose like duties. We must strive to attain permanent relations of confidence, respect, and friendship. Equality must prevail. There must be no coercion; no secret understandings; no conquest; no selfish alliance against the older nations from which we are sprung; no balance of power; no threatening armies. There must be mutual helpfulness; enlarged intercourse; and just law must be the rule of administration between American nations and in American nations. Such was Blaine's conception of Pan-Americanism.[11]

The Meaning of Pan-Americanism

It need only be observed that with respect to the subsequent conferences, which were held at Mexico City in 1902, at Rio de Janeiro in 1906, and at Buenos Aires in 1910, the United States pursued a policy in entire harmony with the principles laid down by Blaine. Not until some years later do we find anything in the nature of a fresh attempt to define Pan-Americanism. It was in his message of December 7, 1915, that President Wilson declared:

> The moral is, that the states of America are not hostile rivals but coöperating friends, and that their growing sense of community of interest, alike in matters political and in matters economic, is likely to give them a new significance as factors in international affairs and in the political history of the world. It presents them as in a very deep and true sense a unit in world affairs, spiritual partners, standing together because thinking together, quick with common sympathies and common ideals. Separated, they are subject to all the cross-currents of the confused politics of a world of hostile rivalries; united in spirit and purpose, they cannot be disappointed of their peaceful destiny.
>
> This is Pan-Americanism. It has none of the spirit of empire in it. It is the embodiment, the effectual embodiment, of the spirit of law and independence and liberty and mutual service.[12]

The chief executives of the United States since Wilson have, without exception, given expression to similar views. None has spoken more forcefully or with greater conviction than Franklin Delano Roosevelt. Announcing his "good neighbor" policy in his first inaugural address, he was able in the second, four years later, to report gratifying progress in the achievement of that ideal.

Among the nations of the Western Hemisphere the policy of the good neighbor has happily prevailed. At no time in the four and a half centuries of modern civilization in the Americas has there existed—in any year, in any decade, in any generation in all that time—a greater spirit of mutual understanding, of common helpfulness, and of devotion to the ideals of self-government than exists today in the twenty-one American republics and their neighbor the Dominion of Canada. This policy of the good neighbor among the

Americas is no longer a hope, no longer an objective to be accomplished. It is a fact, active, present, pertinent and effective. In this achievement, every American nation takes an understanding part. There is neither war, nor rumor of war, nor desire for war. The inhabitants of this vast area, two hundred and fifty million strong, spreading more than eight thousand miles from the Arctic to the Antarctic, believe in, and propose to follow, the policy of the good neighbor.[13]

It remains now to inquire whether the views of the representative men of the other republics of the New World are in accord with those officially set forth in the name of the United States, for agreement is essential to the conception of Pan-Americanism as a union of equal states. The friction and misunderstanding between some of the republics, the anomalous situation which for a time existed in the region of the Caribbean, and the doubts and misgivings in some quarters as to the real aims of the United States, tend to produce a certain reserve among the leaders throughout Hispanic America, which is sometimes interpreted as a sign of indifference or even of an unfriendly attitude toward any idea of American unity. Nothing could be farther from the truth. The best opinion of the southern republics, it may be confidently asserted, is in hearty accord with the authoritative pronouncements of our own statesmen. There are frequent and fierce outpourings in the Hispanic American press, it is true, which are often cited as evidence to the contrary. Upon analysis, however, they prove to be the expression of hostility not to Pan-Americanism, but to what is regarded as the violation of its true principles. The failure to note this fact is usually coupled with the failure to give due weight to more favorable but less insistent views backed by greater authority. Hence the common error of underrating the force of opinion upon which the peculiar American state system rests.

The relations between Mexico and the United States during the decade or more following the downfall of Porfirio Díaz, it must be admitted, can scarcely be regarded as a shining ex-

The Meaning of Pan-Americanism

ample of American unity. It should be remembered, however, that these later years of friction and ill feeling were preceded by a half-century of the most cordial intercourse, due largely to the part the United States played in putting an end to French intervention in Mexico. Taking advantage of the outbreak of the Civil War, Napoleon III found a pretext for landing in Mexico an expeditionary force which was used to overthrow the republic and establish an empire under Maximilian, brother of Francis Joseph, emperor of Austria. At the close of the war in the United States, Secretary of State Seward, by a combination of skillful diplomacy and military threat was influential in causing Napoleon to withdraw the troops. Maximilian, left without foreign support, soon fell and the government of Mexico was restored to the Mexican people.

The years which followed this incident were characterized by unusual manifestations of cordiality between the United States and Mexico. Seward, after his retirement from the office of secretary of state, made a journey to Mexico and was received with every mark of friendship and good will, while Matías Romero, who ably represented the Mexican Republic at Washington during the period of the intervention and for long years afterward, was showered with attentions in the United States. During his residence in the United States Romero never ceased his labors in the interest of friendly relations between the two neighboring republics and in the interest of continental solidarity as well. To his sound judgment and wise diplomacy may be attributed in great part the success of the International American Conference which was held at Washington in 1889–1890. Nor can it be said that his attitude was a matter of mere personal predilection. He undoubtedly embodied the growing spirit of friendliness of the Mexican government and people toward the United States, which spirit continued to prevail until the unfortunate series of events after the fall of Díaz resulted in a state of mutual distrust all but culminating in war. There are happily now signs of returning cordiality on both sides of the Rio Grande, and it is ardently to be hoped that in the future no misunderstandings in this quarter will be allowed to disturb the peace of the American family of nations.

To the superficial view, the relations between Colombia and the United States provide still more convincing evidence of the lack of unity among the American republics. That Colombia has had grievances against the United States growing out of the secession of Panama, is not to be ignored. It is not my purpose to discuss the merits of this question. I shall be content merely to call attention to the fact that Colombia was from the beginning of her existence a champion of American unity. Under the leadership of Bolívar, the republic, then consisting of a federation of Venezuela, New Granada, and Ecuador, launched the first movement of continental union, which in 1826 came to a head in the Panama Congress. Shortly before that assembly took place, John Quincy Adams expressed the fear that unforeseen accidents might baffle all its high purposes and disappoint its fairest expectations. "But," he said, "the design is great, is benevolent, humane."[14] And Clay declared: "The fact itself, whatever may be the issue of the conferences of such a congress, cannot fail to challenge the attention of the present generation of the civilized world and to command that of posterity."[15]

The United States recognized Colombia in 1822. Colombia was indeed the first of the new states to be recognized. Adams gives in his *Memoirs*[16] an affecting account of the simple ceremony of receiving Manuel Torres as the first minister. "The President," says Adams, "invited him to be seated, sat down by him, and spoke to him with kindness which moved him even to tears." That was the beginning of a period of friendly relations which continued without interruption until 1903. Not even then were diplomatic relations severed. In spite of its grievances, Colombia remained an active member of the American concert, though with a certain reserve altogether natural under the circumstances. After the long-pending treaty in-

The Meaning of Pan-Americanism

tended to restore the former cordial relations between the republics went into effect, Colombia reverted to the same active, enthusiastic support of Pan-American unity which characterized its foreign policy in days gone by.

In the countries south of the Equator, we find public opinion more outspoken, less subject to the restraints imposed by international friction such as mars the relation between the United States and some of the Caribbean republics. Of these southern states none has been a more ardent advocate of continental unity than Brazil. And yet during the hundred years of its independence Brazil has had abundant occasion for conflict with the surrounding countries. On its northern, western, and southern borders it touches every state in South America except Chile and perhaps Ecuador. This vast frontier, in the beginning vague and ill defined, gave rise to numerous boundary disputes, all of which, greatly to the credit of the states concerned, have been satisfactorily adjusted. In the early years, it is true, Brazil was involved in armed conflict with the Argentine Confederation, and later with Paraguay. Fortunately, however, these conflicts left no lasting bitterness and today the republic enjoys to a marked degree the good will and affection not only of these neighbors, but also of the other republics throughout the continent.

With the United States the relations of this greatest of the southern republics have always been of the most friendly sort. As early as 1824 Brazil officially declared the Monroe pronouncement to be applicable to all the states of the continent. It recognized the necessity of unity in the defense of American rights and in the defense of the integrity of American territory. Nearly a hundred years later, just after the United States entered the World War, we seem to hear an echo of these same sentiments in the words of the Brazilian ambassador at Washington. "The republic," he declared, upon informing the State Department of the break of his government with Germany, "thus recognized the fact that one of the belligerents is a constituent portion of the American continent and that we are bound to that belligerent by traditional friendship and the same sentiment in the defense of the vital interests of America and the accepted principles of law." To this he added that the events which brought Brazil to the side of the United States were imparting to her foreign policy a practical shape of continental solidarity."[17]

Brazil, moreover, has invariably lent powerful support to the Pan-American movement as expressed in the International American Conferences. While still an empire it sent delegates to the first conference at Washington, and while that conference was in session the bloodless revolution which changed its form of government took place. The delegates then at Washington continued as representatives of the republic. Some years later the third conference was held at the Brazilian capital, on which occasion the government and people manifested in unmistakable form their loyal adherence to the principles of Pan-American unity. Senhor Nabuco, president of the conference, and for many years Brazilian ambassador at Washington, declared that the purpose of the conferences was the creation of an American opinion and an American public spirit. He believed that the conferences should never aim at forcing the opinion of a single one of the nations taking part in them; that in no case should they intervene collectively in the affairs or interests that the various nations might wish to reserve for their own exclusive deliberation. "To us," he said, "it seems that the great object of these conferences should be to express collectively what is already understood to be unanimous, to unite in the interval between one and another what may already have completely ripened in the opinion of the continent, and to impart to it the power resulting from an accord amongst all American nations."[18]

Two years later Senhor Nabuco was a speaker at the laying of the cornerstone of the magnificent building of the Pan American Union at Washington. He declared on this occasion

The Meaning of Pan-Americanism

that there had never been a parallel for the sight which that ceremony presented—"that of twenty-one nations, of different languages, building together a house for their common deliberations." To this he added: "The more impressive is the scene as these countries with all possible differences between them in size and population, have established their union on the basis of the most absolute equality. Here the vote of the smallest balances the vote of the greatest. So many sovereign states would not have been drawn so spontaneously and so strongly together, as if by irresistible force, if there did not exist throughout them, at the bottom or at the top of each national conscience, the feeling of a destiny common to all America."[19]

The little Republic of Uruguay has left no doubt as to its attitude. In an address on the occasion of Elihu Root's visit to Montevideo in 1906, the president, Señor Battle y Ordoñez, declared that America as a whole should aim at the ideal of a just peace founded on respect for the rights of all nations; that a Pan-American public opinion should be created and made effective by systematizing international conduct, with a view to suppressing injustice and establishing among the nations ever more and more profoundly cordial relations; and finally, that the Pan-American conferences were destined to become a modern amphictyon to whose decisions all the great questions would be submitted.[20]

Shortly after the United States entered the World War, Admiral Caperton with a fleet of war vessels paid a visit to Montevideo. The relations between Uruguay and Germany were at that time strained almost to the breaking point and the fleet was received with extraordinary manifestations of friendship. The cabinet passed a resolution, which was subsequently published as a presidential decree, declaring that, whereas the Uruguayan government had on various occasions proclaimed the principle of American solidarity, "no American country which, in defense of its own rights, is in a state of war with nations of other continents, shall be treated as a belligerent."[21] *El Día,* a leading daily of the Uruguayan capital, approved the action of the government, declaring: "America is one. Everything unites it; nothing separates it." That these were not merely the expressions of wartime enthusiasm is evidenced by a carefully prepared plan suggested by President Brum in the spring of 1920 for the organization of an American League of Nations on the basis of absolute equality, which he proposed should act in harmony with the League of Nations under the Covenant of Versailles.[22]

The Argentine Republic succeeded in maintaining neutrality throughout the World War and naturally no official pronouncements such as those made by Brazil and Uruguay during that period are to be expected. Moreover, we should not fall into the error of regarding a break with Germany as a test of Pan-Americanism. Solidarity, it is true, is of the essence of Pan-Americanism; but no less essential to the conception is the principle of noninterference, which is made effective not by collective obligation but by individual responsibility. The United States, guided by its traditional policy, refrained from participation in the conflict until it was compelled to act in defense of its rights. On similar grounds, Brazil was impelled to declare war and Uruguay to break off diplomatic relations with Germany. The expressions which I have quoted above were incidental to the abandonment of neutrality, and likewise the absence of such declarations on the part of the Argentine government can be accounted for by its adherence to neutrality. Public opinion as voiced in the press of Buenos Aires was predominantly American in sympathy. Argentina in recent years has been among the staunchest supporters of the basic principles of Pan-American policy. In the words of one of the most eminent of her sons, Luis M. Drago, America seeks power and wealth not "in conquest and displacement, but in collaboration and solidarity." "It has been constituted," he maintains, "a separate political factor, a new and vast theatre

The Meaning of Pan-Americanism

for the development of the human race, which will serve as a counterpoise to the great civilizations of the other hemisphere, and so maintain the equilibrium of the world."[23]

A territorial dispute, usually referred to as the Tacna-Arica question, growing out of the war between Chile on the one side and Peru and Bolivia on the other, for a generation disturbed the peace between these nations and caused more or less concern throughout the continent. There was reason, however, to hope that the question in the process of adjustment would furnish another proof of the effective unity of America. Indeed, in the diplomatic correspondence which resulted in the agreement between Chile and Peru to enter into direct negotiations at Washington with a view to the final settlement of the dispute, striking evidence was given, on both sides, of what may be called a Pan-American consciousness. In one of his communications to the Chilean government, the minister of foreign relations of Peru, referring to the fact that the government of Chile had declined to recognize the jurisdiction of the League of Nations over the question on the ground that it was an American political problem, proposed "in the interest of American cordiality" that the whole matter should be submitted to arbitration at the initiative of the United States. On both sides, as the interchange of communications went on, such expressions as "the welfare of our two nations and of America as a whole," and "in the interest of American peace and concord," repeatedly occurred, demonstrating a decent respect for the opinion of the whole community of American nations. The settlement of the dispute was finally achieved by direct negotiations, with the friendly coöperation of the United States. The outcome redounded to the prestige of Chile and Peru and justified all the expressions of continental interest and good will.[24]

The Chaco war of recent memory furnishes, paradoxical as it may seem, another illustration of continental solidarity. When Bolivia and Paraguay a few years ago appeared to be about to resort to war over disputed boundaries in the Chaco region, the nineteen other American nations interposed their good offices in the hope of bringing about an amicable adjustment. This friendly action succeeded in postponing, though not in averting, the war; but the failure did not deter the mediating governments from further efforts. Persistently and with infinite patience they continued to intercede, in one combination or another, until at last, in June, 1935, the ministers for foreign affairs of Bolivia and Paraguay signed, at Buenos Aires, in the presence of the representatives of the mediating powers, a protocol by the terms of which the belligerents agreed to settle their differences by direct negotiation, or, if that failed, by arbitration.[25]

It was at this conjuncture of affairs that President Roosevelt suggested the peace conference which met at Buenos Aires in December, 1936. The opportunity was favorable, the President thought, for the American republics "to consider their joint responsibility and their common need of rendering less likely in the future the outbreak or the continuation of hostilities between them, and by so doing, serve in an eminently practical manner the cause of permanent peace on this Western Continent." The proposal met with instant acceptance and all the republics, including the two recently at war, sent representatives to participate in the conference. As the deliberations were harmonious, the achievements were correspondingly gratifying. Among other things, the conference subscribed to an important declaration of principles, reaffirmed the existing peace agreements, and approved a new convention binding the signatories, in the event of future threats of war, to consult together with a view to preserve the peace of the continent.[26] To this advance in the organization for peace the Chaco war had undoubtedly contributed.

To present the subject at greater length from the Hispanic American point of view would make the case no more convincing. Suffice it to say that the sober, responsible, representative

The Meaning of Pan-Americanism

opinion of the states of Spanish and Portuguese origin finds itself generally in accord with the best opinion in the United States. On the other hand, the contrary views, varying from mild skepticism to the bitterest opposition, which are often met with in the public press not only of the Hispanic American countries but of the United States as well, should not be ignored. Though seldom proceeding from authoritative sources, yet these hostile expressions have a plausible basis in certain acts of alleged aggression on the part of the United States, and to a less degree perhaps in disputes between other states of the continent. The complete disarming of the critics of Pan-Americanism can only be accomplished by removal of all causes for distrust. This is a task to which the statesmen of both continents should devote their most earnest attention.

An attempt must now be made to bring the loose threads of this discussion together into a concise description of Pan-Americanism. As to its *genus*, the lexicographers give us a choice among the following: tendency, aspiration, idea, principle, doctrine, advocacy, sentiment—none of which satisfies. Former Secretary of State Lansing suggests another. Pan-Americanism, he says, is a policy—an international policy of the Americas. This seems to assume some Pan-American agency, such as the International American Conferences, to formulate the policy. But what we conceive to be Pan-Americanism seems to lie back of these conferences. It seems to be, in relation to them, cause rather than effect. The conferences, Ambassador Nabuco truly said, merely express collectively what is already felt to be unanimous.

There is another way of viewing the matter which may bring us nearer the true meaning of Pan-Americanism. Wilson speaks of the American states as constituting a "unit in world affairs"; Cornejo, of a "continental system"; Drago, of a "separate political factor"; and Moore declares that Pan-Americanism is obviously derived from the conception that there is such a thing as an American system. This idea is inherent in the Monroe

Doctrine, and it found expression two years before Monroe's pronouncement in a speech of Clay's in which he declared that it was in our power to become the "center of a system which would constitute the rallying point of human wisdom against all the despotism of the Old World." Such also was the basic idea of Bolívar's Panama Congress. This view of America as a separate political factor is not confined to the Western Hemisphere. European observers recognize it, and in textbooks of international law, such as that of T. J. Lawrence, one may find the "American State System" discussed at length. This takes us back to the conception of Pan-Americanism as involving some sort of union.

If, then, there is an American system, an American society of nations, there must be the beginnings of an international American government; for a group of states cannot live together without some semblance of government. But government implies constitution; that is, a collection of principles formally expressed or not, according to which the powers of government and the rights of the governed and the relations between the government and the governed, are adjusted. There has been developed thus far in America no definite, tangible organ of international government. The International American Conferences may be considered as such, if at all, only in the vaguest sense of the term. The Pan American Union, with its magnificent home in Washington, cannot be so considered; for it is little more than a bureau, nonpolitical in character. Back of this bureau, however, and back of the International American Conferences, there is a moral union of the American states, based upon a body of principles which have, in the course of the years from the struggles for independence to the present time, become more or less clearly defined. To these principles we must turn for the meaning of Pan-Americanism. They are:

1. *Independence.* By this is meant complete political separation from Europe, the American states neither interfering in

The Meaning of Pan-Americanism

the affairs of the European states nor allowing those states to interfere in their own affairs. If the lines of political connection with Europe had been maintained, obviously there could have been no American state system, and naturally no Pan-Americanism.

2. *Representative government.* The fact that all American states have cherished from the beginning of their existence a common political ideal, the ideal of popular, representative government, has been and is a powerful bond of union between them. The practice of American governments, to be sure, is not always in accord with the rule. But governments pass; ideals endure.

3. *Territorial integrity.* The states of this hemisphere are a unit in declaring that conquest is inadmissible in American public law. The fact that the boundaries between the Hispanic American states remain today practically as they were determined by the *uti possidetis* of 1810 is evidence of the force of this principle. The repeated declarations of the United States to the effect that it neither covets the territory of its neighbors nor seeks to aggrandize itself by conquest give additional sanction to the rule.

4. *Law instead of force.* There is no balance of power in America, no group of powerful states imposing its decisions by force upon weaker states. Action in the International American Conferences is taken by unanimous consent, and this rule precludes the development of a balance of power. The spirit of just law, as Blaine expressed it, is the rule of administration between American states.

5. *Nonintervention.* This follows as a corollary of the foregoing principle. The American states as a body have never undertaken to intervene in the affairs of any particular state. Through the American Institute of International Law they have officially declared that "every nation has the right of independence in the sense that it has the right to the pursuit of happiness and is free to develop itself without interference or

control from other states." From the strict observance of this principle the American states as a body have never departed. The United States individually has on occasion intervened, but not in a spirit of denial of the principle; rather at bottom and ultimately to maintain it unimpaired.

6. *Equality.* Not only do the American states recognize equality as a principle of international law, but in the conduct of their international conferences they observe it to the fullest extent, presenting in this regard a striking contrast to the European practice. In respect of certain of the weaker republics, it is true, the United States undertook for a while the exercise of international police power the effect of which was to infringe apparently the equality of the states concerned. But as in the preceding case, the ultimate aim was to maintain rather than to deny the principle.

7. *Coöperation.* Friendly coöperation in the advancement of common political, economic, and cultural interests is a notable characteristic of the American state system. The Pan American Union at Washington, itself a striking example of coöperation, provides an agency for the further promotion of coöperation, an agency the transcendent importance of which we have hardly as yet begun to realize.

Upon these foundations Pan-Americanism rests.

Diplomatic Futility

Futility marked the early relations of the United States with Central America. Nothing went right; everything went wrong. The very agents of the Washington government seemed to move under an evil star. Physical hardships, vexations of spirit, dread diseases, and in some cases death itself attended them. Of the eleven appointees before 1849, three died *en route;* another succumbed before he started on his mission; one escaped with his life by being dismissed before he embarked; another survived by contriving to draw his salary for more than a year without going near the Central American capital; and another traveled over the length and breadth of the country, unable to find a government to receive him. Though the remaining four reached their destination and were received, only one of these prolonged his stay beyond a few months, and he committed suicide soon after his return to the United States.

Nor is this the whole story of adversity. The country to which the ill-starred agents were accredited, was itself the victim of misfortunes of the greatest magnitude. Organized in 1824 under a constitution similar to our own, the Central American federation was confronted from the beginning by obstacles which it could not surmount. No strong sentiment of nationality bound the parts together; communication was slow and difficult; the mass of the population was ignorant and indifferent; many of the upper class were frankly reactionary; and the leaders of the enterprise were themselves torn by conflicting personal interests. Civil war, secession, foreign encroachments, political chaos, and a whole train of accompanying evils left the country hopelessly prostrate.

Misfortune on the one hand; disaster on the other. Is it possible that some fatal connection existed between the two? It is evident that the elements of salvation for the Central American republic did not lie within itself. Could external aid have saved it from destruction? The United States alone was in a position to render this friendly office; yet it failed utterly to perform its neighborly function. Was the failure a mere matter of mischance, the result of unforeseeable and inevitable misfortunes? Could it have been caused, in part at least, by a certain unawareness at Washington of the nature and magnitude of the Central American problem? In part by ignorance of the climatic, topographic, and social conditions which prevailed in the new state? In part by diplomatic awkwardness? In part by the subservience of diplomacy to party politics? Perchance by a combination of a number of such causes? Let the somber details speak for themselves.

The first agent designated was Thomas N. Mann of North Carolina. Bred to the law and limited in outlook to the horizon of his native state, he was ignorant of the language, customs, and institutions of Spanish America, and even of the very location and extent of the country to which he was to be sent. Be it said to his credit, however, that he was eager to learn. Immediately after his appointment in April, 1824, he went to Washington and had interviews with President Monroe and Secretary of State Adams. He wanted enlightenment not only on the geographical, social, and political conditions of Central America, but on matters of high personal interest to himself: he wanted to know by what means he was to reach his destination, and how long his exile in that far country was to continue. On this last point Adams, whose duty it was to satisfy the agent's curiosity, appears to have had nothing to say. Perhaps he had a premonition that talk of returning from Central America before one arrived was a bit premature. On the other points the secretary of state was more explicit, though in matters of detail he was himself somewhat confused.

I told him [says Adams] of the principal objects of his mission: that the first of them was to obtain and transmit information respecting the country to which he was going—a new central South

Diplomatic Futility

American, and as it would seem, confederated republic, situated at and including the Isthmus of Panama, a position of the highest geographical importance—in̄ ortant also by the commercial connections, and lodgements on the soil by the British, with the neighboring Bay of Honduras and Mosquito Shore. It was furthermore interesting from the step once taken by St. Salvador, now forming a portion of the republic, to connect itself directly with the United States. It was understood that one of the deputies who came here on that occasion was now, or recently had been at the head of the new Guatemalan Government. By the public newspapers it appears that they had appointed a public Agent or Minister to come to the United States. The republic bordered on those of Mexico, Colombia, and Peru; but our information concerning it was scanty, and we expected to receive much from his Agency.[1]

Adams's information was obviously scanty. It did not greatly matter, however, that the new republic did not extend to South America nor include the Isthmus of Panama; for, reduced to its proper limits, it occupied nevertheless a position of the highest geographical importance. It did not matter that the British at the moment had no lodgement on its soil; for they did have an establishment at Belize which served as a base for commercial connections, and as a point of departure for later territorial encroachments, including a reassertion of old claims on the Mosquito Shore. It did matter that Adams hit upon two of the essential elements—geographical importance and lodgements of the British—of what in years to come was to be known as the Central American question. His mention of the proposed annexation was intended to convey some notion of the friendly reliance of the weak on the neighborly protection of the strong. This amicable relationship was to form the basis of a third element of the question; that is, championship, by the United States, of the Central American cause.

Unfortunately, Adams did not clearly apprehend the significance of a unified and stable republic of Central America as a factor in the contest which he vaguely foreshadowed. Neither in his conversation with Mann nor in his formal instructions,[2]

---
[1] Superior figures refer to notes on pages 164–165.

which were but an elaboration of the main points of the interview, did he propose any steps to aid the leaders then engaged in framing what to them was a strange form of government. This was the time to render assistance; but the golden opportunity was allowed to pass. When the real meaning of the federation was finally perceived, the good offices of the government at Washington were powerless to prevent dissolution or to effect restoration. Internal chaos and foreign aggression were the result.

How to reach Guatemala was a perplexing question. The prospective traveler could not avail himself of any regular sailings to the Central American coast, for there were none. He could occasionally obtain passage to the Isthmus of Panama, but his progress from there northward on the Pacific was extremely uncertain. He had even less opportunity in these days to go by the Nicaragua route, for vessels seldom touched at San Juan del Norte. Of the other more or less direct ways, the only one open to him was the trail which led inland from Izabal, farther up the coast, on the Golfo Dulce. But to get to Izabal was a problem. If he had the good fortune to be taken aboard by a ship going in that direction, perhaps after a roundabout course, he had to disembark at Omoa on the coast of Honduras or at the British port of Belize, to continue his voyage on a chance vessel of light draft capable of navigating the shallow waters of the gulf. Delays at every point, exposure to the diseases prevalent on tropical shores, and the discomforts of the land journey from Izabal onward rendered his undertaking arduous and perilous to the highest degree.

Mann knew little of these matters, and in his ignorance he applied to the Department of State for assistance. But to Adams the subject was annoying. It irked him to attend to such details. "These private economies of our public Ministers and Agents," he confided to his diary, "are among the most disagreeable appendages of my public duties."[3] Yet the harassed secretary went through with the unpleasant task, and while Mann returned to North Carolina to attend to private business and prepare his "baggage and library" for shipment, Adams succeeded in arranging the desired passage on the United States ship of war *Hornet*, soon to depart on a cruise in southern waters. Two months later Mann embarked at Norfolk, and the *Hornet* turned its prow, not toward Omoa or Belize, but toward La Guaira, Venezuela. Other interests took precedence, and as the vessel cruised Mann fell sick and died on board.[4] His mission ended before it had well begun.

William Miller, also of North Carolina, and a former governor of that state, was designated in March, 1825, as Mann's successor. He was commissioned as chargé d'affaires, recognition having been accorded the Central American federation in August of the preceding year. His instructions were ready in April, exactly a year after the date of Mann's appointment.[5] Two months later Miller was in Washington seeking aid of the Department of State in reaching the Central American capital. Whether the memory of Mann's fate on board a public vessel had anything to do with the matter or not, the new agent was left to make his way as best he could by such means as chance might afford. Accordingly he sallied forth and for months was lost to view. How he traveled, what difficulties he encountered, and what hardships he endured the records do not reveal. They only show that he reached Key West, and that there he fell, in September, 1825, a victim of yellow fever.[6]

John Williams of Tennessee, the next in order, was more fortunate. At the time of his appointment, in December, 1825, he was in the prime of a vigorous manhood. His career had been active and varied. At the age of twenty-one he was a captain in the United States infantry; at twenty-five he was admitted to the bar; at thirty-four he raised a regiment of mounted volunteers, and by conducting a successful campaign against the Seminoles won a commission as colonel in the regular army. After serving throughout the War of 1812, he was elected United States senator from Tennessee, and in this capacity remained at Washington until 1823. He was one of General Jackson's bitterest adversaries, which explains at once his descent from the Senate and his elevation to a diplomatic post. If he had been less valiant he might have quailed before the mission to Central America. But his courage was a matter of record: he had faced death on the battlefield, and for good measure he had defied Andrew Jackson. It was no wonder that such a man should be the first to reach Guatemala and return alive.

In March, 1826, three months after his appointment, Williams was at Norfolk awaiting passage on the sloop of war *John Adams*. In April he was at Havana, and in May he reached Guatemala. But this was six months after his appointment, and a full two years after the first agent's appointment. Precious time had been lost. We learn from Williams's communications that the federation was already in a process of dissolution; that the federal and state governments were in constant collision; that the house of deputies, recently in session, had adjourned without passing the appropriation bill; that a forced loan was being talked of; that seizure of church property was contemplated; that a territorial dispute with Mexico threatened war; and that the British were extending their trespasses. Williams warned the Central American officials that their country was on the brink of an awful gulf, and he recommended as a possible means of salvation the adoption of the writ of habeas corpus, trial by jury, and Livingston's Louisiana code. He urged also the founding of a national bank with a metallic basis, and on request drew up a charter for such a bank. These were, after all, mere devices, and Williams had little hope of seeing the republic saved from destruction. "They have no master workmen among them," he said, "& the whole machinery is badly contrived." Under conditions so disheartening, he made his stay short. In December, six months after his arrival, he turned the affairs of the legation over to the acting consul, and set out on the return journey to the United States.[7]

Diplomatic Futility

William B. Rochester of New York was commissioned in March, 1827, to succeed Williams. He it was who managed to reap the fruits of office without rendering any useful service. He was an adept in this art. For nearly a year he had been the recipient of a salary as secretary of the mission to Panama without budging from his native state, and at the time of his appointment to the Central American post, he was in Mexico to attend a second meeting of the congress, which never materialized. Under his instructions for the new post, which he received in May, 1827, he had two courses open before him: he could go promptly to Guatemala and assume the duties of his office; or, if his private affairs demanded, he could first visit the United States, and then proceed to his destination.[8]

Rochester had, it must be admitted, an intellectual perception of the nobler course. He had been told by agents of the Central American republic in Mexico, so he wrote the secretary of state, that the situation was urgent; that the departure of Colonel Williams had been viewed with great regret; that the government and people were most friendly toward us; and that it was their sincere desire to cultivate and maintain a good understanding with our country.[9] His fervent account leaves us almost convinced that his emotions were touched, and that his sense of duty was aroused. He informed the secretary of state that it was his intention to go to his post at once; and he made his way promptly down to Vera Cruz, to proceed by way of the Bay of Honduras for Guatemala. But the flesh was weak. He embarked instead for New Orleans,[10] and once there he was loath to quit again his native soil.

The movements of Rochester during the next year were amazingly dilatory. From New Orleans, where he arrived early in June, 1827, he wrote that having failed to obtain an early passage to the coast of Central America, he had resolved to send his baggage to New York, from which city he would sail after paying a visit to his family. In July, he was at the ancestral home in Rochester; in September, he spent some days in New

York, where he professed to be making preparations for his departure; in October, he was back at Rochester; in November, he missed sailing from New York on the *John Adams;* in December, he promised to "use due diligence in getting to Norfolk by means of steamboats & stages" to meet the sloop of war *Falmouth,* in which he now proposed to sail; in January, he was in Washington where the President could observe his snail-like pace; in February, his perseverance brought him to Norfolk; and in March he at last embarked. After a long and restful cruise on the *Falmouth,* he went ashore, in May, at Omoa. Here he faltered still. Instead of hurrying on to the Central American capital, three hundred miles away, he embraced the first opportunity to take passage for the United States. In June, he was back, and in October his diplomatic career was closed with commendations from the secretary of state.[11]

This strange affair becomes stranger still on examination. Rochester owed both his appointments to family connections with Secretary of State Clay.[12] In itself this is not remarkable. Public servants have often been selected on such grounds, and thus selected have frequently failed to render any corresponding service. But the acquiescence of the austere and correct President in proceedings so sterile and so oblique is beyond belief. Adams knew that Rochester while nominally secretary of the mission to Panama was busily engaged in efforts to promote the political interests of Henry Clay in the state of New York; he knew that to permit Rochester, after a brief and fruitless residence in Mexico, to travel over half a continent before assuming duties that lay close at hand was a waste of public funds and a damage to the public interest; he knew that Rochester's delay in New York during the summer and fall of 1827 was still in the interest of party politics; and finally, he knew that Rochester set out in the spring of 1828 with no intention of establishing a residence in Central America. The following excerpts from Adams's *Memoirs* bear witness to these facts,

Diplomatic Futility

though they do not remove our wonder that the President could actually have been a party to conduct so reprehensible.

January 8, 1828. Mr. Barnard, a member of the House of Representatives from New York, came with Mr. Rochester, the Chargé d'Affaires to the Central Republic of Guatemala, who is going with lingering step to Norfolk, to embark for the port of his destination. This gentleman was at the last election of Governor of New York a candidate for that office against DeWitt Clinton, and has an earnest craving to be a candidate again.... But upon the vulgar adage, "a bird in the hand is worth two in the bush," he goes to Guatemala, looking back to New York—like Reynolds's picture of Garrick, between Tragedy and Comedy.[13]

March 19, 1828. Mr. Brent came from Mr. Clay, and mentioned that Mr. Rochester, the Chargé d'Affaires to the Central republic of Guatemala, was still at Norfolk, waiting for his passage. By the accounts recently received from that country, a desperate civil war is raging among them; and Mr. Clay proposed giving an instruction to Mr. Rochester, if he should find upon his arrival at Omoa that no useful purpose would probably be attained by his proceeding to his destination, to return immediately to the United States.

I assented to this, but desired Mr. Brent to present to the consideration of Mr. Clay the expediency of suspending for the present the mission to Guatemala and directing Mr. Rochester not to proceed on the voyage.... Mr. Clay was here.... He spoke of Mr. Rochester, and thought it would be most expedient to instruct him to proceed to Guatemala, the letters from the Consul at Omoa, Phillips, expressing much solicitude for his arrival, in the hope that his presence might afford protection to the persons and property of our citizens there. Mr. Rochester has been so long at home, waiting for a passage, that Mr. Clay thought it would be more satisfactory to him, and also to the public mind, that he should go to the place of his destination, rather than that his mission should now be abruptly terminated. But he agreed that it would be advisable shortly to abolish the mission to the central republic; and rather because he had this day received a letter from Mr. Gonzales, their Chargé d'Affaires in this country, now at New York, announcing that in consequence of the disastrous state of his own country he found himself compelled to embark for home....[14]

June 23, 1828. Mr. Brent sent me several dispatches, received since Mr. Clay's departure yesterday morning—among them letters from William B. Rochester, Chargé d'Affaires to Guatemala, who has returned and landed at Savannah. The republic of Central America is in a state of Civil War, and the Government is virtually dissolved...."[15]

July 7, 1828. Mr. Southard brought me a bundle of letters and enclosures from Master-Commandant Charles W. Morgan, commander of the sloop-of-war Falmouth, just arrived at Pensacola, from a cruise in the Gulf of Mexico and the Caribbean Sea. This vessel was sent to take W. B. Rochester ... and John Mason, Jun., the Secretary of Legation to Mexico, to the countries of their respective destinations. He landed Rochester at Omoa, but, instead of proceeding to his post, he posted off to the British settlement in the Bay of Honduras, and thence back to the United States, where he arrived some time sooner than the Falmouth, which carried him out. Morgan, in a private letter to Mr. Southard, intimates that Mr. Rochester was quizzed into very unnecessary panic by a British Agent at Omoa, and describes his agitation and movements in a manner somewhat ludicrous. Rochester's masterpiece of diplomacy seems to have been in changing his ships, and coming back in a different vessel from that in which he went out.[16]

The office of chargé d'affaires to Central America was now left vacant for a while. The Adams administration ran its course and two years of the reign of Andrew Jackson passed before a successor to Rochester was appointed. In the meanwhile Clay yielded the office of secretary of state to Martin Van Buren and Van Buren to Edward Livingston. It was Livingston who was responsible for the restoration. His long residence at New Orleans, where his gaze was constantly directed toward the south, his knowledge of the language, customs, and institutions of Spanish America, his preparation of a universally praised code of laws thought to be peculiarly adapted to the needs of the new republics, his exceptional opportunities for observation, and his habit of intelligent reflection on the phenomena presented to his view gave him a profound understanding of Central American problems and a sure grasp of the importance of the region to the world in general and to the United States in particular.

Diplomatic Futility

The reasons assigned by the preceding administration for discontinuing all efforts to maintain contact with the crumbling republic did not appeal to Livingston. He set his hand with zest to the preparation of fresh instructions, in which he substituted for the earlier vague generalities clear-cut and specific injunctions. He gave "geographic importance" a concrete meaning. He made it signify a transisthmian ship canal—a stream of interoceanic commerce—and an awakened Central America with free ports, good roads, and a growing trade, from all of which the United States, because of its proximity to the scene and because of the enterprise, the wealth, and the proficiency of its citizens, would derive great advantages. And in closing his instructions he touched with feeling upon the peculiar regard which Central America merited as a neighbor and sister republic.[17]

But neither time nor Livingston's fresh enthusiasm brought better luck. The new agent, William N. Jeffers of New Jersey, appointed in June, 1831, set forth, but got no farther than Pensacola. There he was overtaken by ominous communications. Accusations against him had been lodged at the Department of State, and when, after some months of interchange of correspondence, the matter came to a head, Jeffers resigned[18] his commission to disguise virtual dismissal.

A worse fortune befell his successor, James Shannon of Kentucky. He accepted the appointment and set out on the hazardous journey with a hopefulness which passes all understanding. Accompanied by his wife, his son Charles, and his niece, Miss Shelby, he embarked in June, 1832, at Pensacola on the sloop of war *Vincennes*. After a short and uneventful voyage, he landed at Omoa, where he expected to take passage for Izabal. Disappointed in his expectation, he availed himself of an opportunity to pass with his retinue across to Belize, whence the superintendent, Colonel Cockburn, sent the party forward— unwittingly to a tragic dénouement. At Izabal James Shannon and Miss Shelby were stricken with yellow fever, and within a few days both were dead. The survivors laid the bodies to rest in the damp soil, and, burdened with sorrow, returned by way of Belize and New Orleans to their home in Kentucky.[19]

No perfectly normal person would now accept the post. Charles G. DeWitt of New York State, who did accept it, was undoubtedly a bit queer. It required six months of search to find him and agree upon his appointment, and nearly twice as many months of prodding to get him past Shannon's grave and on to Guatemala. The story would be amusing if it were not so pathetic. DeWitt was appointed in January, 1833, and being "extremely anxious to depart," went to New York City for that purpose. In April he wrote that he was still detained for the "want of an opportunity to proceed." It is not unlikely that something else besides the want of opportunity detained him. Perhaps the dismal history of the previous attempts to reach the fatal city had come to his ears. He was not so mad as to walk deliberately into the jaws of death. Shannon's grave at Izabal was a warning symbol. Was it not possible to avoid the perils of this route? Assured by persons well acquainted with the country and the climate that the "safest, surest and most prudent course" was around Cape Horn, he engaged passage on the ship *Leonidas,* bound for "Valparaiso, Lima and Central America."[20] Would not the President and secretary of state lend their approval?

DeWitt doubtless had not sufficiently pondered the effect his longest-way-round plan would have on the stern soldier who sat in the White House. Old Hickory's methods were direct. Dangers did not deter him. Safety and prudence were not in his vocabulary. Exactly what he said about DeWitt's proposal we do not know. Perhaps it would not be fit to print if we did. The record we have is the softened paraphrase in a letter of Livingston's.

He [the President] directs me to inform you that he very much regrets that the circumstance of your lameness [for DeWitt was lame] will make it inconvenient for you to go to your destination

Diplomatic Futility

by the usual route; but that he cannot by any means approve the project of making the voyage to the South Seas, round Cape Horn, in order to get to Central America, a place almost at our doors.— You could not in framing the plan, have attended to the distance, and to other circumstances that would render it entirely inconvenient to you, and impossible to be sanctioned with propriety, by the government—You would have first, 170 Degrees of latitude to sail in a southern and a northern direction, and 70 or 80 of longitude in the different courses you will be obliged to pursue in order to arrive at a place to which you would arrive in the direct course, by going less than 30 degrees—Add to this, that when you arrive at Valparaiso you will be twice as far from your destination as you are now, and with infinitely fewer opportunities of reaching it.[21]

This rebuke had a slight galvanic effect, and DeWitt engaged passage on a vessel soon to sail. But, detained by illness, he did not embark. In July, he wrote: "You shall hear from me as soon as my health is reestablished. In the meantime, in the name of humanity, do not hurry me off before I am fit to go." In August, he gave details of his illness: "From the 2nd of May till the middle of June, I lay on my back, a mere lump of clay—a plague to myself, and I presume a greater plague to others." Fortunately "by the blessings of God and the skill, care and attention" of his physician he survived. All of which left the obdurate President untouched. In September, another reprimand, more scathing than the last, was administered. The poor ailing man was reminded that the appointment, made long months ago, had been "dictated by the necessity of speedily renewing our intercourse with Central America," and he was given to understand that the sincerity of his desire to achieve that object was a matter of doubt in the mind of the President. This was effective. In October, the laggard agent, browbeaten and abashed, set sail in a merchant vessel for Kingston, Jamaica, where he arrived after nineteen days of sufferings which he would not "undertake to describe." In November, a British packet took him to Belize, and in December he rode into the city of Guatemala.[22]

Some incidents of his journey are worthy of remark. At Belize he met with a cordial reception from "His Excellency, Francis Cockburn, the Governor," who not only sheltered the forlorn traveler but offered a vessel and crew for the voyage to Izabal. "The impression which such godlike benevolence has imprinted in my mind," wrote DeWitt, "may be imagined but cannot be described." Poor fellow! He is never able to describe. He leaves so much for us to imagine. And we do imagine. Harsh words from Washington, whence kind words were due; friendliness at Belize, where animosity might have been expected. DeWitt wins our sympathy and then our admiration. He was not a robust, gallant, intrepid individual. He was on the contrary delicate of health, lame, shrinking, timid. He dreaded the hardships and dangers along the way. Yet, under pressure, he met them with fortitude. At Izabal he paid a visit to the last resting place of his lamented predecessor, Shannon, and, depressed by the wild appearance of the spot, procured a young orange tree and planted it at the head of the grave. This sacred duty performed, he proceeded through tropical jungles and over difficult mountain trails to his destination. Every foot of the way was painful. Not only that, says DeWitt: "I was three times thrown from the mules—once at the hazard of my life."

Five long years DeWitt continued at his post. He did not run true to form and hasten back. Singularity, quirk, twist, aberration—something—marked him off from the common herd. It may have been nothing more than a desire of escape, of self-effacement. It may have been inertia. It may have been a sense of duty. Or it may have been dread—dread of pain, dread of sickness, dread of death on land or sea. We cannot be sure, for DeWitt was strange. For a while his behavior seemed normal. He wrote regularly, giving the State Department such information as he was able to gather. But he seemed not to be fully aware of his environment. He spoke too much of tranquillity when there was none. His Central American view was limited

Diplomatic Futility

by the mountains that surrounded Guatemala City. He did not sally forth. He was lame, and he shrank from the hazards of the road. He vegetated. After four years he wrote and meekly asked for leave to spend a few months in the United States. He was told in substance to come home and resign. This hurt. He had to explain that his object was serious, that he wanted "to visit a sick wife confined for months to her bed." Then Washington relented and granted him leave, which he would not for some time take advantage of. "The roads leading from the capital," he declared, "have for the last six weeks been so infested by armed bands of highwaymen, that no prudent traveller, and least of all a foreigner, will venture to set out for any distant point." And prudence kept him on more than a year longer.[23]

In DeWitt's absence changes had taken place at Washington. The old martinet who hated prudence had returned to Tennessee to spend his declining days at the Hermitage. Van Buren was in his place. Livingston had long since yielded his office to Louis McLane, and McLane had been succeeded by John Forsyth. But DeWitt reaped no profit from these changes. Scolding him had become a habit and he was welcomed with words of reprobation. He had been told not to leave his post until he had negotiated a renewal of the treaty which had been concluded with Central America in 1825 and which was now about to expire by its own limitations. He had violated his instructions. He had come home without the treaty. Disobedience so flagrant must be punished, and he was ordered to face again the perils of the road to Guatemala. He was to acknowledge his failure and do penance by going back to take proper leave of the Central American government and to bring the mission to a formal close.[24] He could not make the State Department understand that his failure was excusable; that he had done all anyone could do in the circumstances; that he had secured signatures to the renewal but could not get the document ratified, simply because the congress, the ratifying body, had ceased to function; that to incur all the risks involved in the return trip for the purpose of taking leave of a phantom government would be worse than useless. How disheartening! Forever driven, forever harassed, he had never received a word of kindness, of appreciation, or of commendation from his superiors. The world was cold, full of troubles and hazards and pain. And poor DeWitt chose to leave it by his own hand.[25]

Four of the seven appointees thus far designated had been claimed by death. Still another, William Leggett, a native of New York City and sometime editor of the famous *Evening Post*, was to make the supreme sacrifice. He was appointed to do what DeWitt had rebelled against doing; that is, he was to go to Guatemala to close the luckless mission. Unfortunately he was already seriously ill, and his appointment appears to have hurried him on to his grave. Before the ink was fairly dry on his commission his earthly career came to an end. Whereupon the government, nothing daunted, selected a new agent in the person of John L. Stephens. Though born in New Jersey, Stephens, like Rochester, DeWitt, and Leggett, was appointed from New York. But he was not like his confréres in any other respect. He was not a shirker to evade the task laid out before him; he was not a hypochondriac to nurse his ills; nor was he an invalid on the verge of the grave. He was indeed better equipped than any of his predecessors had been to undertake the mission. He was a man of superior intelligence; he had initiative; he knew men and affairs; and he was experienced in travel. Moreover, he was proficient in antiquarian studies, and this, together with his desire to explore the little-known vestiges of the ancient civilizations of Central America, caused him to enter upon the enterprise with singular enthusiasm. Alas! he was to deal with ruins only; for the federation of Central America, like the Mayan régimes before it, had ceased to exist.

Within these limitations Stephens succeeded where others failed. That is, he reached Guatemala City, performed the last sad rites over the defunct mission, traveled widely over the

Diplomatic Futility

country, made hasty but important archaeological investigations, and returned to the United States without succumbing to disease. Accompanied by an English artist, Frederick Catherwood, he sailed from New York in October, 1839, on a British vessel bound direct for Belize, and, meeting with no delays, landed there within the month. The new superintendent of the settlement, Colonel Macdonald, received him with cordiality, and thus heaped up the debt of our gratitude to Belize. Nowhere else in this region were the British so amiably disposed toward the Americans. At Guatemala, indeed, the British consul general, Chatfield, sowed seeds of dislike toward us, and these seeds in the course of time germinated and grew and produced bitter fruit. Belize was a place of hospitality. The Shannons had been the recipients of its benefits, and Mrs. Shannon and her son, who returned to it after the tragedy at Izabal, had cause to remember it with melancholy gratitude. DeWitt found its benevolence impossible to describe. Happily, Stephens suffered from no such disability. His account of the farewell dinner with which he and Catherwood were honored leaves us with a vivid sense of the reality of the settlement as a friendly haven for the American pilgrims who passed that way.

The large window of the dining room opened upon the harbour [says Stephens]; the steamboat lay in front of the Government House, and the black smoke, rising in columns from her pipe, gave notice that it was time to embark. Before rising, Colonel M'Donald, like a loyal subject, proposed the health of the Queen; after which he ordered the glasses to be filled to the brim, and, standing up, he gave, "The health of Mr. Van Buren, President of the United States," accompanying it with a warm and generous sentiment, and the earnest hope of strong and perpetual friendship between England and America. I felt at the moment, "Cursed be the hand that attempts to break it"; and albeit unused to taking the President and the people upon my shoulders, I answered as well as I could. Another toast followed to the health and successful journey of Mr. Catherwood and myself, and we rose from the table. The government dory lay at the foot of the lawn. Colonel M'Donald put his arm through mine, and, walking away, told me that I was going into a distracted country; that Mr. Savage, the American consul at Guatimala, had, on a previous occasion, protected the property and lives of British subjects; and, if danger threatened me, I must assemble the Europeans, hang out my flag, and send word to him. I knew that these were not mere words of courtesy, and, in the state of the country to which I was going, felt the value of such a friend at hand.[26]

Fortunately, Stephens had no occasion either to hang out his flag or to call for help; but he ran many risks and suffered hardships enough. At Izabal he saw the English engineer of the little steamer that had brought them into the Golfo Dulce, a man of Herculean frame, fall ill and lie helpless as a child. He remembered that he had been told that Izabal was a sickly place, and that it was running the gauntlet for life even to pass through it. He remembered, too, what he had strangely forgotten, that Shannon lay buried there; and he, like DeWitt, sought out the burial place, finding it on "a rising ground, open to the right, stretching away to the Golfo Dulce, and in front bounded by a gloomy forest." He also was depressed by the desolate spot, and ordered a fence to be built around the unmarked grave.[27] Moreover, his friend "the padre promised to plant at its head a cocoa-nut tree." Cocoanuts and oranges! Whether DeWitt's young orange tree or the padre's cocoanut tree ever grew to drop their fruit in respectful homage on Shannon's grave, we do not know. Later passers-by tell us nothing. Rank tropical vegetation no doubt promptly claimed the lonely place and hid it forever from human view.

Stephens ran the gauntlet of fever at Izabal to encounter other hazards on the road. He and his party, mounted on mules and heavily armed, set out in the wake of a caravan of pack animals on the way to Guatemala. Passing a marshy plain, they soon entered an unbroken forest where the mules sank deep in puddles and mudholes. As they advanced, the shade of the trees became thicker, the holes larger and deeper, and roots, rising two or three feet above the ground, crossed the path in every direction. At the foot of the Mico Mountains, over which they had to pass to enter the valley of the Motagua, the ascent began precipitously through a narrow gully, worn by the tracks of mules and the washing of mountain torrents. Beyond this defile they encountered still deeper mudholes and larger roots, with the additional difficulty of a steep ascent. The woods were of impenetrable thickness, the rain poured, and there was no view except that of the detestable path before them. Stephens reflected that perhaps their inglorious epitaph might be, "tossed over the head of a mule, brained by the trunk of a mahogany tree, and buried in the mud of the Mico Mountain." Indeed all were tossed—Catherwood with such violence that Stephens, who witnessed his fall, was horror-struck. The servant's mule fell backward, and then followed such a rolling and kicking on the part of man and beast that it seemed quite marvelous that nothing more serious resulted than a thorough plaster of mud for both. Stephens himself, when his turn came, by straining every nerve flung himself clear of roots and trees and barely missed impalement on his dagger, which had fallen from its sheath and stood with its foot of naked blade upright in the mud.[28] Enough for one day—the first day—and enough to convince us that DeWitt could not have been guilty of exaggeration when he averred that he had been thrown three times on the whole journey. Indeed, in all the circumstances we are inclined to think that his "once at the hazard of my life" must have been a modest understatement of the facts in the case.

We cannot follow Stephens through all his adventures in Central America, for they were many and varied. At every turn he was exposed to perils. Not the least serious among them were those of which he had heard at Belize—the perils growing out of the distracted state of the country. On the way up to Guatemala, in spite of his official character, he was put under arrest and threatened with death by the ignorant and ruffianly alcalde of a wayside village; and at various points along the route he was saved from the violence of bandits by his own calm judgment and unflinching courage. Arriving at the capital he found the whole city in a state of awe. The term of the federal officers had expired some months before and no elections had been held to supply their places. Salvador and Quetzaltenango alone clung doubtfully to the federal idea, and Morazán, the champion of that cause, had abandoned the capital and now held momentary sway in Honduras. Carrera, an Indian, supported openly by a ragged and fanatical mob and covertly by the reactionary elements of the upper class, was master of Guatemala. The atmosphere was charged with hostility for foreigners. It had been some months before that the United States consul, Charles Savage, performed the act which won the admiration and gratitude of Colonel Macdonald. On the occasion of an assault on the house of a British subject, one of the leading merchants of the place, Savage, as Stephens heard and related the incident, "rushed down the street under a shower of bullets, knocking up bayonets and machetes, drove the mob back from the door, and, branding them as robbers and murderers, with his white hair streaming in the wind, poured out such a torrent of indignation and contempt, that the Indians, amazed at his audacity, desisted." As yet there had been little change for the better. Only a few days before Stephens's arrival the British vice consul had been insulted and his flag fired upon.[29] These acts seemed to be the expression of enmity not merely toward the British, but toward all foreigners. It was a dangerous state of affairs, yet the American representative passed through it all without suffering bodily harm.

Immediately after his arrival he took possession of DeWitt's house. On first viewing it he had been favorably impressed by its external appearance, and on entering he was charmed with its interior. It was one of the finer residences of the city. Other houses of the capital were larger, "but mine," said Stephens, "combined more beauty and comfort than any habitation I ever saw." Yet, ensconced in an official residence, he had no official duties to perform. His credentials were addressed to a nonexistent government, and unless Morazán, who still pur-

Diplomatic Futility

sued the forlorn hope, should meet with success, it would become necessary to secure the archives, dispose of such property as could not be conveniently shipped to the United States, and close the legation. But Stephens did not sit in vain impatience awaiting developments. Central America lay before him with a thousand enticements, and he responded to its allurements. He traveled and observed, beginning with little journeys from Guatemala City as a base, and then extending his excursions to more distant parts of the country. From the Pacific coast of Guatemala, where he burned with fever and shook with ague, he embarked for Costa Rica, and on the voyage he lay in a hammock recuperating, and amusing himself by reading *Gil Blas* and *Don Quixote*. He traveled to the Costa Rican capital; ascended the volcano of Cartago, from which point he could view both the Atlantic and the Pacific; returned to the coast and journeyed northward on muleback; studied the Nicaragua Canal route in passing; visited old cities; climbed threatening volcanoes; rode through the whole length of Salvador; and, on his way to Guatemala, met Morazán in utter rout before the fierce warriors of the Indian Carrera.

Convinced of the hopelessness of the federal cause, he put aside all idea of acting in an official capacity and devoted himself to archaeological investigations. He had already turned aside on his way up from Izabal to make a reconnaissance of Copán; and, during his absence in the south, Catherwood had descended the Motagua and examined the ruins of Quiriguá. The two of them now set out along the great Guatemalan plateau, and entering the Mexican province of Chiapas, paused at Palenque to explore the highly interesting ruins in the neighborhood. Continuing their journey to the Gulf of Mexico, they went by water to the northern coast of Yucatán, and made a preliminary survey of a number of ruined cities there. They then set sail for New York. Rich in experience and laden with notes and drawings, the travelers returned to their starting point. They had been gone a little less than ten months, and within an even smaller space of time Stephens issued from the press, in two volumes, a fascinating account of their travels. Stephens's narrative, with its easy-flowing style, its vivid descriptions, and penetrating observations, together with Catherwood's excellent drawings portraying the little-known monuments of a vanished civilization, gave the work an instant success. Edition after edition was called for, and thus the public, as well as the Department of State, acquired welcome though belated information about Central America.

What became of Stephens? The answer is that Central America enchanted him, and though it spared him for a time, at last it lured him to his death. As soon as his book was published he returned to Yucatán, accompanied as before by Catherwood, to carry forward his archaeological investigations. The fruit of the new expedition was another work[30] no less felicitous than the first. After this he was elected a member of the New York State constitutional convention, and at about the same time he joined others in organizing the first American transatlantic steamship company. Then he became interested in the Panama Railroad Company and was successively its vice president and president. This enterprise kept him for some time on the Isthmus, where his health, already undermined by his previous travels in Central America and Yucatán, at last gave way, and he passed to his reward at the untimely age of forty-seven.

The fragile and often broken thread must be taken up again. When Stephens disposed of DeWitt's paraphernalia and quit the Central American capital to wander among older and more interesting ruins, the break seemed to be final. But we never know what Washington will do. With William Henry Harrison in the White House and Daniel Webster at the State Department, it changed its mind. It heard rumors of a revival of the Central American federation, and, yearning for authentic information, designated William S. Murphy of Ohio as a "Special Confidential Agent" to go out and obtain it. Murphy's movements were relatively expeditious, and his sufferings,

Diplomatic Futility

though great, were not beyond his powers of description. Appointed in July, 1841, he reached Guatemala before the end of the year, "very sick of a fever taken on the road." Some weeks later he wrote: "I dislike apologies . . . but the chills and fever with which I have been afflicted . . . have greatly retarded my labors." These remarks were at the end of a thirty-five-page legal cap letter.[31] And he wrote other long reports. How much "authentic information" he might have provided if he had been at his best, is a subject upon which it would be futile to speculate.

Of one thing we may be certain: he could not have found any indication of a reviving federation, for there was none to find. On the contrary, every sign pointed in the opposite direction. In the lucid intervals between his attacks of malaria, Murphy could see that. He could see, too, that the reactionary elements in control were falling more and more under British influence, and that a corresponding sentiment of hostility toward the United States was being developed. He learned of the advantage the British were taking of the situation to make encroachments on the northern coasts of Honduras and Nicaragua and of the tendency of those countries to look to the United States for protection against British aggression. In short, he saw and traced for the Department of State the main outlines of the Central American question, now for the first time beginning to take definite form. Having done this—three months were required for the task,—he escaped to the United States. But tropical disease apparently got him at last. He died during an epidemic of yellow fever in Galveston, a year or two later, while on a diplomatic mission to the Republic of Texas.[32]

Six years passed before the United States called upon another of its sons to travel the dangerous road. Loath to admit the failure of the general government of Central America, the authorities at Washington were equally reluctant to recognize the existence of independent states within the territory once embraced in the single federation. Moreover, the energies of the northern republic, particularly in the Polk administration, were directed toward the acquisition of territory and the fixing of boundaries in the west. There were difficulties enough in that direction without rushing into new ones in the south. The British were free therefore to strengthen their hold on Guatemala, to ingratiate themselves with Costa Rica, and to seize such positions between these two states as were deemed essential for the control of interoceanic communication. As soon as the successful termination of the Mexican War seemed assured, however, the attention of the United States was turned once more toward the isthmian region. In March, 1848, Elijah Hise of Kentucky was commissioned as chargé d'affaires to Guatemala and empowered to conclude a treaty with Salvador. To this extent only was the dissolution of the federation acknowledged, no decision being made as to the status of the other countries formerly members of the union. Washington still hoped for the restoration of the federation, and if Hise found sentiment favorable he was to help bring it about.[33] He was not, however, to challenge the British; for, the treaty with Mexico not having been concluded, it was deemed unwise for the moment to bring the Central American question to an issue.

Hise chose the Panama route. The records do not show what considerations entered into his choice. It could hardly have escaped his notice that two good Kentuckians already lay moldering in the ground at Izabal; and as he was to be accompanied by his wife, and a nephew—Kentuckians all,—he may have been moved by the patriotic desire of conserving the noble strain to which he and they belonged. Unfortunately, he was not possessed of the pathfinding instincts of his forebears, and in his efforts to avoid a perilous road on the one hand he ran into a worse one on the other. On the voyage southward, early in the summer following his appointment, his ship was wrecked on one of the small islands of the Baha-

Diplomatic Futility

mas, and passengers and crew were forced to live for ten days on the barren spot in tents made of the sails of the disabled vessel. He had the good fortune, however, to find the means of continuing his voyage to the Isthmus. In three days, by the aid of canoe and the inevitable mule, he crossed with his suite to Panama; after which, he confessed, he and his family were indisposed. Weeks passed and no vessel sailed for the coast of Guatemala. In the meantime indisposition developed into serious illness, and as Hise's body suffered, his spirits sank. The Isthmus became a place of horror. Izabal could be no worse. In desperation he returned by a "dreadful and most hazardous" journey to Chagres, and sailed for Jamaica, where he expected to fall in with a vessel bound for the Bay of Honduras.

From Jamaica he wrote a doleful account of his sufferings; but he was not disposed to give up the mission. He had determined to send his wife and nephew back to the United States and then proceed by sea to the "Gulph of Dolce," from which, he declared, "I will if I live make my way by land to Guatemala." Yet he had the feeling that too much was expected of him. "If the mission is important," he complained, "the Govt. should enable me to get there or recall me." While waiting in Jamaica he was again prostrated with fever "and brought to the verge of the grave." Reduced to a mere skeleton, he "tottered on board" a vessel bound for Havana, where he expected to find an opportunity to proceed on his journey; but he thought it was "due to truth and candour" to say that he almost despaired of reaching his destination alive. He expressed the hope that on account of the wretched state of his health the President would conceive it proper to recall him. Then, as if by magic and much to the credit of Havana, his health improved. He embarked for Omoa. On the way, his health continued to improve, and as his spirits rose correspondingly, he began to ponder on the destiny of his country. "By the by," he volunteered, "I should like to say something on the Cuba Question. A question upon which I think I am pretty well informed, but it would be out of place here; I would certainly give my support most cordially to an administration that should be in favor of—and knew how *to* EFFECT the ANNEXATION of Cuba to the United States."[34] It mattered little now that twenty days were required to sail from Omoa to the Golfo Dulce, and it mattered less that his vessel went on the rocks before it reached Izabal. The traveler was well, his wife and nephew were safe at home, and the dangers ahead seemed of little consequence. After six months of wanderings and of torment our agent came happily to his destination.

He achieved little. While he peregrinated in the Caribbean, the party in power at Washington went to the polls and lost. Three months after he reached Guatemala, the new administration took over the reins of government. Hise was then recalled; but as he did not for some time receive the letter communicating the fact, he remained at his post until the following summer. During his residence, which was thus extended to seven or eight months, he divided his time with perfect impartiality between the things he was authorized to do and the things he was not authorized to do. He concluded a commercial convention with Guatemala, in accordance with his instructions; and he tried to negotiate a similar convention with Salvador, also in accordance with his instructions. But this was dull work. What fascinated him was the forbidden challenge to England. He had not long been in Guatemala when he wrote the secretary of state: "It is clear to my mind that Great Britain designs to become the owner and occupant by force or stratagem of the ports on the Atlantic and Pacific coasts of Nicaragua which will be the points of termination of the canal communication between the two oceans."[35] Later he wrote: "English agents and influence under the experienced direction of the British Consul Genl. Fredk. Chatfield are alive and at work both in C. A. and at London to produce results most inimical to the U. S. and to embarrass and obstruct any negotiations here. I have reference to the Mosq. question."[36]

Diplomatic Futility

Under conditions so provoking how could any chivalrous American refrain from throwing down the challenge to Great Britain? Hise could not. Authority or no authority, he could not stand idly by and see weak nations overridden by a mighty power, and, incidentally, his own country deprived of a free crossing place to the Pacific. He entered into correspondence with the victims—inspirited them, urged them to resist the wicked designs of the British nation. Nicaragua being an especial object of his solicitude, he urged its government, with warm words of encouragement, to look to the great republic of the north for protection. "I say to you," he declared, "that the United States hopes and desires that the state of Nicaragua will stand on her rights, and that she may not for a moment consent to yield to the Diplomatic arts that may be practiced or the threats of hostility which may be uttered by Great Britain a single foot of her rights of Territory & Dominion in and upon the Mosquito Coast & Country and over the River and Port of San Juan de Nicaragua."[37] It so happened that Nicaragua was in the mood to throw itself into protecting arms. Accordingly, it sent a commissioner to negotiate with Hise. The result was a canal convention by the terms of which the United States was obligated to guarantee the sovereignty of Nicaragua over territory which the British stood ready to defend in the name of the Mosquito king. This was the challenge. But it never became effective. The new administration at Washington pursued a course of conciliation, not of challenge.[38] Hise had his trouble for nothing.

In the best of circumstances, there was little that any United States agent could do; for Central America had fallen under the dominion of Britain. Though it was almost at our doors, its approaches were guarded by the British outposts of Jamaica and Belize. Its flanks—Guatemala and Costa Rica,—while American forces slept, had surrendered to British direction and control. Its Atlantic shore line, embracing the eastern terminus of the Nicaraguan canal route, had become in effect British territory under a thin Mosquito mask. Its Bay of Fonseca, dominating the western terminus of the route, lay under the guns of British warships. Its whole extent of land and waters was under the observation of British officials. Its very existence as a single state was subject to British whim. In the achievement of all this there had been no muddling through: no aimless, wanton aggression; no dying of agents *en route;* no floundering on the road. Everything had been done effectively and in proper season. Everything had been foreseen and prearranged. Every move in the north had been met by a countervailing move in the south. The field of battle had been prepared. The British were at their posts.

Such was the Central American situation in 1849; such the result of a quarter of a century of diplomatic preparation on the part of Great Britain; such the result of a quarter of a century of diplomatic futility on the part of the United States.

The Pan-Americanism of Blaine

JAMES G. BLAINE occupies a place of great importance among the promoters of Pan-American unity. It is to the period of the Civil War that one must go to discover the influences that gave him his peculiar bent. Incidents of those years make intelligible, if they do not wholly justify, the distrust which, it must be confessed, he entertained in some degree toward certain of the Old World powers, particularly Great Britain, France, and Spain. His Anglophobia, if such it may be termed, was inspired by what he believed to be British partiality for the Southern cause.[1] This aroused in him a feeling of resentment, which fortunately time and the friendly settlement of the *Alabama* claims largely removed.

France and Spain had likewise given cause for offense in Blaine's eyes. They had taken advantage of the preoccupation of the United States to flout the Monroe Doctrine—an offense which a good American finds it difficult to condone. Under French protection the Second Empire had been established in Mexico, and Maximilian, archduke of Austria, induced to ascend the throne, where he was maintained by French bayonets. Spain, disappointed in the part which it hoped to play in the intervention in Mexico, sought compensation by reincorporating Santo Domingo in its national territory, and on a flimsy pretext went to war with the Pacific states of South America in the hope, doubtless, of making further conquests in that quarter. To the disillusionment of the Spanish American countries, England had complacently looked on.[2]

These aggressions the United States was unable to prevent. Its resources were being expended in a colossal effort to thwart a dissolution of the Union. It protested, but mildly; it declined to recognize Maximilian, but without hostile gestures; it continued to deal with the patriot government of Juárez, but

---
[1] Superior figures refer to notes on page 165.

without ostentatious partiality. It bided its time, and when the Civil War was over, it succeeded by a diplomacy which had force in the background in hastening, if not compelling, the withdrawal of the French troops from Mexican soil. Maximilian speedily fell and the government of Mexico was recovered by its people. Spain also turned back. The sovereignty of the Dominican Republic was restored, and the war in the Pacific came to a futile end.

The moment was opportune for reviving the fraternal spirit which had prevailed among the states of the New World during the second and third decades of the century, and which later had been all but destroyed by the aggressive tendencies of the United States temporarily under the obsession of manifest destiny. Much of the fear and distrust aroused during that exuberant period had been removed by the outcome of the Civil War; for to the slave states had been attributed the imperialistic trend of the nation. With slavery gone and the Union restored, Latin America looked again to the United States as a friendly protector against European encroachments. On our side, we had been chastened by our sufferings. The arrogant, impatient attitude that we had assumed towards our turbulent neighbors had yielded to a measure of sympathy and understanding. Had we not shed more blood in four years to settle internal difficulties than they in forty years? Did we not owe them gratitude for the unmistakable evidence which they had given of their desire for the preservation of the Union? Under these changed conditions it was possible to begin building anew on just and lasting foundations a permanent structure of international American good will. That Blaine saw and made use of this opportunity is his chief title to lasting fame.

In Blaine's own words the foreign policy of the Garfield administration, which he had joined as secretary of state, had two objects: "First, to bring about peace and prevent future wars in North and South America; second, to cultivate such

The Pan-Americanism of Blaine

friendly, commercial relations with all American countries as would lead to a large increase in the export trade of the United States, by supplying fabrics in which we are abundantly able to compete with the manufacturing nations of Europe."[3] The attainment of the first object was a prerequisite to the accomplishment of the second. Blaine's idea was to cease depending on partial measures—friendly interventions, patched-up treaties, ineffectual truces. Permanent peace, he believed, could be attained only by means of a comprehensive plan, and to this end he proposed to enlist the good will and active coöperation of all the states of the Western Hemisphere in a general congress to be held at Washington. He did not immediately extend invitations to the congress, for there were difficulties in the way. A war involving Chile, Peru, and Bolivia was raging in South America, and nearer at hand hostilities threatened between Mexico and Guatemala. Concord among these states must first be restored.

The Mexico-Guatemala dispute was of long standing. It grew out of conflicting claims to the province of Chiapas, which in colonial times had been attached to the captaincy general of Guatemala. In 1821 both Guatemala and Chiapas, acting separately, joined Mexico. On the fall of Iturbide, in 1823, Guatemala withdrew, with Mexican consent, to unite with Honduras, Salvador, Nicaragua, and Costa Rica in the short-lived Republic of Central America. Chiapas elected to remain a part of Mexico. The Guatemalan contention was that the province had been coerced; Mexico took the position that its choice had been free. In the meantime the province remained under Mexican control.

In his desire to contribute to a friendly adjustment of the dispute, Blaine was influenced in a measure doubtless by a chivalric regard for the weaker contestant. He disclaimed partiality, it is true. Yet he was pleased to have Guatemala make formal application to the United States, "as the natural protector of Central American integrity," to use its good offices to bring about a peaceable settlement; and he gave heed to information received from Central American sources to the effect that Mexico was plotting to precipitate hostilities with a view to extend its borders far beyond the territory in dispute. Blaine feared that in a war so unequal, successful resistance on the part of Guatemala would be impossible, and that the other Central American states would become involved, which would result in their defeat and eventual absorption in the Mexican federal system. Thus we should have on this continent "another lamentable demonstration of the so-called right of conquest," which would postpone indefinitely "that sympathy of feeling, that community of purpose, and that unity of interest upon the development of which depends the future prosperity of these countries."[4]

Not only did Blaine wish to avoid the evils that would follow in the train of conquest, but he desired also to prevent the complications that would inevitably arise if some European power should intervene in the quarrel, as he had reason to believe would occur if Guatemala were driven to extremities. He accordingly urged that the conflict be averted by diplomatic means, or, these failing, by resort to arbitration. The Mexican government did not receive his suggestion with favor. It believed that he had been instigated to interfere by Guatemala, and that he had therefore prejudged the case. Undiscouraged, he returned to the charge with new arguments and more urgent appeals; but without avail. Insistence served only to irritate. His proposal of arbitration, at first politely declined, was now indignantly rejected as officious interference. Blaine truly had cause to be exasperated, but he remained calm and conciliatory. In his last dispatch on the subject he expressed deep regret that Mexico should be unwilling to join the United States in establishing the principle of friendly arbitration of international differences on the American continent.[5]

When Blaine left the State Department, this dispute stood about as he found it. His successor did not press the matter, and Guatemala, no longer feeling that it had the support of a powerful friend, entered into direct negotiations with Mexico, as a result of which a settlement was arrived at some months later substantially in accordance with the Mexican contention.[6]

Simultaneously with his endeavor to effect a settlement between Mexico and Guatemala, Blaine was striving zealously to restore peace between the belligerents in South America. Here likewise he failed to attain his immediate aim, and the conflict, already in its second year, dragged on for three years longer. The heritage of hatreds, and of angry bickerings over still unsettled questions growing out of this war, abundantly justifies the efforts which Blaine so persistently made to interpose his good offices in the interest of a just and lasting peace.

The War of the Pacific grew out of a territorial dispute. When the Spanish American colonies began their revolt from the mother country, they tacitly adopted a rule which was intended to preclude conflicting territorial claims. This was a rule based on the Roman principle of law known as the *uti possidetis*. It provided that the new states should conform to the limits of the major administrative divisions existing in 1810, the year when Spain ceased to exercise over its American possessions full and undisputed authority.[7] The rule was generally observed; but in some regions the boundaries were so indefinite that disputes inevitably arose. This was the case in the desert of Atacama. There had never been in colonial times any necessity for determining exact lines of demarcation in that uninhabited and barren waste. Peru ended vaguely on its northern borders, and Chile began no less vaguely on its southern limits. In between, Upper Peru, destined to become later the Republic of Bolivia, thrust a strip of uncertain width to the Pacific. These haphazard frontiers the three republics inherited, and for some years no occasion arose to give them clearer definition.

Toward the middle of the century, interest in the neglected region was awakened, for it was found to be rich in mineral resources, chief among which was nitrate of soda. Boundaries were no longer a matter of indifference. The *uti possidetis* of 1810 acquired a new interest for the possessors of this storehouse of wealth. Old documents were brought forth and reëxamined in support of the varying claims. On the north, Peru and Bolivia were able to agree on a dividing line marked by the Loa River, which flows into the Pacific at about 21 degrees 30 minutes south latitude. Farther down the coast, the claims of Bolivia and Chile overlapped. By treaty in 1866 the two countries set the boundary conditionally at latitude 24 degrees south. In 1874 this boundary was confirmed by a second treaty, which stipulated that neither party would impose within the territory formerly in dispute any taxes in excess of those already fixed by law. Claiming that Bolivia had violated the agreement, Chile seized, in February, 1879, the Bolivian port of Antofagasta. Bolivia immediately replied with a declaration of war against Chile. In consequence of a secret treaty of alliance, which it had concluded with Bolivia in 1873, Peru soon became involved in the war.[8]

The outcome of the contest was dependent on sea power. Bolivia had no navy, and its population was concentrated in the high plateau beyond the Andes, at a great distance from the scene of conflict. Difficulties of transportation alone put the country at a tremendous disadvantage. It could neither save its coast provinces nor render effective assistance to its ally. Peru, after the first few months of the war, confronted Chile alone. Its cruisers for a time held the enemy in check, but finally succumbed to the growing power of the Chilean navy, and the whole Peruvian coast lay open to attack. First Tarapacá, richest of the nitrate fields, then Tacna and Arica, yielded to the vigorous Chilean onslaught. Progressively the operations moved up the coast. A well-equipped army was concentrated about Lima, and in January, 1881, it forced the surrender of that important city. Except for desultory fighting, the war was at an end.

At the moment of its defeat Peru had no government with which the victor would treat. In the midst of the war the constitutional régime had been set aside and Nicolás de Piérola had been proclaimed dictator. On the fall of Lima he escaped with a remnant of his forces to the interior, whence he made various ineffectual attempts to open peace negotiations with the Chileans. An effort to end this anomalous situation resulted in the establishment, under Chilean protection, of a provisional government with Francisco García Calderón as president. This government was recognized by the United States in the hope of facilitating peace negotiations.[9] Chile, however, never fully recognized it; indeed, later the Chilean authorities became hostile to Calderón and took him away a prisoner to Santiago.

Thus matters stood when Blaine assumed the duties of secretary of state. The opportunity for the peacemaker was an alluring one. If the United States could find the means of reestablishing harmonious relations between the belligerents, its prestige as the friend and counselor of the American nations would be greatly enhanced, and the way to the adoption of a comprehensive peace plan would be made relatively easy. As in the Mexico-Guatemala dispute, Blaine's chief concern was to prevent annexation of territory by conquest. He had reason for anxiety, as the Chilean government had officially declared that the cession of Antofagasta and Tarapacá as a reimbursement for the expenses of the war was an indispensable condition to the negotiation of peace.[10] From this demand Chile showed no signs of receding, though it stoutly contended that the war was not one of conquest.

In writing his first full instructions on the subject, Blaine recognized the *fait accompli*. The United States, he said, could not refuse to acknowledge the rights which the Chilean government had acquired by the successes of the war. Annexation of territory might be the necessary price to be paid for peace; but it should be made as a result of negotiations, not of conquest. It would be injudicious therefore for Peru to declare that it would in no circumstances cede a part of its national domains, and he hoped that Chile, since it had distinctly repudiated the idea that the war was one of conquest, would not demand the cession of territory as a condition precedent to peace negotiations. A meeting of minds on this basis would be possible. The points at issue would then be a proper indemnity to Chile, and suitable guaranties for the maintenance of peace in the future. Whether Peru would be able to make any arrangement at home or abroad that would furnish the necessary indemnity or supply the required guaranties, was uncertain; but if it could do so without sacrificing the integrity of its territory, the United States would tender its good offices for the execution of such a project. If no plan could be devised for meeting the reasonable conditions of Chile, the exaction of territory as a prerequisite to peace would become a fair subject of consideration.[11]

The recipients of these instructions were Stephen A. Hurlbut and Hugh Judson Kilpatrick. Both were veterans of the Civil War, in which both attained the rank of major general; both had served for a time immediately after the war as ministers to South American countries, and both had recently been called back to the service and were proceeding on their missions as ministers to Peru and Chile respectively. Unfortunately the parallel does not end here. Both became partisans of the countries to which they were accredited; both muddled their instructions, destroying all hope of an early peace; and, finally, both died at their posts, Kilpatrick two weeks before Blaine's resignation, Hurlbut three months afterward. Their appointments were both unfortunate. The ministers whom they superseded, Thomas A. Osborn in Chile and Isaac P. Christiancy in Peru, had been on the ground from the beginning of the conflict, were thoroughly familiar with all its details, had kept the Department of State well informed of the course of events, and had generally performed their duties with ability and discretion. If they had not been recalled, the unhappy complications which ensued might have been avoided.

The ill success of his ministers induced Blaine to try a new plan. The whole matter of the peace negotiations he now entrusted to William T. Trescot, a highly accomplished professional diplomatist, who was appointed as special envoy, with the rank of minister plenipotentiary, to the republics of Peru, Bolivia, and Chile. In his instructions to Trescot, Blaine left much to the envoy's discretion. There were two points, however, upon which he spoke positively. First, in regard to the extinction of the Calderón government, if Trescot should find that the Chilean government had been moved to that act by resentment toward the United States for its continued recognition of Calderón, he was to say that the United States regarded the proceeding as an "intentional and unwarranted offense,"—"an act of such unfriendly import as to require the immediate suspension of all diplomatic intercourse." Secondly, if Chile refused to allow the formation of any government in Peru which did not pledge its consent to the cession of territory, Trescot was to express "in language as strong as is consistent with the respect due an independent power" the disappointment and dissatisfaction felt by the United States at such a "deplorable policy." Indemnity and guarantees, he repeated, Chile had a right to claim, but annexation as a condition precedent to negotiations would be conquest and dangerous to the best interests of all the republics of this continent.[12]

Trescot's mission was doomed to fail. Before he reached his destination, an inauspicious change took place in Washington. Frelinghuysen succeeded Blaine at the State Department. Unwilling to follow the vigorous course traced by his predecessor, he began curtailing Trescot's powers by new instructions. When the Senate called for the correspondence relating to the attempt to bring about a peace, Frelinghuysen sent everything, including the instructions to Trescot and other communications of the most confidential sort. It is difficult to escape the conviction that the object was to expose Blaine—to discredit him before the American people. Shamelessly the peace and welfare of sister republics were thrown into the balance of partisan politics. The correspondence was republished in Chile, with the editorial comments of newspapers in the United States hostile to Blaine, and the impression was created that his policy had excited among his countrymen a strong popular opposition, and that the government was now engaged in explaining away what was deemed objectionable.[13] Under these circumstances, Trescot's presence in South America was worse than useless.

What Trescot might have accomplished if he had not been rendered powerless by Frelinghuysen is a matter of speculation. Given his diplomatic ability and the moral support of a great nation behind him, it is not too much to suppose that he would have brought about a negotiated adjustment far more satisfactory to all parties concerned than the dictated and unstable peace which was finally made. Indeed, Trescot met with an initial success which held out great promise for his mission. Arriving in Chile some three or four weeks before Frelinghuysen's countermanding orders reached him, he began negotiations under his original instructions. Upon his assurance that the United States had no "intention to suggest any solution which would compromise the honor, endanger the true interest, or wound the susceptibilities of either of the belligerents," diplomatic discussions were begun under conditions of the greatest cordiality. The Chilean government disclaimed intentional offense to the United States in the arrest of Calderón, accepted the good offices that Trescot was authorized to extend, promised to facilitate communication with the provisional government of Peru, and proposed conditions of peace. The conditions were hard, but Trescot thought they might be modified by the earnest remonstrance of the United States. At this point came the hampering instructions of Frelinghuysen, and Peru and Bolivia were left to their fate.

The Pan-Americanism of Blaine

On still another point Blaine was reversed. His plans for assembling a Pan-American congress at Washington were rudely set aside. Three weeks before his resignation he had extended the invitations, with President Arthur's concurrence. The harmony that was thought to be a prerequisite to such a conference had not been attained, but the date was set sufficiently far in advance to allow for the adjustment of pending differences. The single purpose of the congress—to consider methods of preventing war between the nations of America—made a strong appeal, and acceptances soon began to arrive in Washington. Then Frelinghuysen, in a dispatch which was published, forecast the abandonment of the project. He doubted whether "partial confidence," extended to "selected friendly nationalities," would conduce to peace.[14] Blaine was greatly exasperated and addressed to the President a public letter of remonstrance, in which he protested that if the congress was renounced on the ground that it would offend the powers of Europe for the nations of America to meet to discuss their own affairs, the United States would be deeply humiliated, would lose the friendship of its neighbors, and would add nothing to its prestige in the European world. He begged the President, therefore, not to permit the government to assume a position so contrary to our traditions and so derogatory to our self-respect. The President was unmoved. After submitting the proposal to Congress, without evoking an expression of views, he instructed Frelinghuysen to withdraw the invitations.

Hostility to Blaine did not end with the reversal of his foreign policy. Once more he was harassed by having his personal integrity questioned. Shortly after the publication of the Chile-Peruvian correspondence, charges were made that one or more ministers who served under Blaine were improperly connected with business transactions in which the intervention of the United States was being sought. The House Committee on Foreign Affairs was ordered to make an investigation. It was clear enough that the chief, no less than the subordinates, was on trial. When called before the committee, Blaine submitted cheerfully to examination, and answered all questions fully. Numerous other witnesses were summoned, and hundreds of pages of testimony were taken. Having failed, after six months of minute inquiry, to uncover any official wrongdoing, the committee made its report. As Blaine was not technically under investigation, no reference was made to him by name; but it was declared that there had not been the "slightest intimation or even hinted suspicion" that any officer in the Department of State had at any time been personally interested in any of the transactions.[15]

In his testimony before the committee Blaine had an opportunity to bring to public view one of the strongest motives for his interest in the War of the Pacific; namely, his desire to prevent European interference. The nationals of England, France, and other Continental powers had important financial interests in the belligerent countries, and Blaine feared that unless the conflict was brought to a speedy conclusion, one or more of those powers would find occasion to intervene. The war had its origin, he believed, in the machinations of these private interests, particularly the British. "It is a perfect mistake," he said, slightly off his diplomatic guard, "to speak of this as a Chilean war on Peru. It is an English war on Peru, and I take the responsibility of that assertion. Chile would never have gone into the war one inch but for her backing by English capital." Outside influences caused the war, and outside pressure would be necessary to bring it to an end. "I think it will be demonstrated in the very near future," he declared, "that the United States will have to assume a much more decided tone in South America than the one which I took and which was rescinded, or else it will have to back out of it, and say that it is a domain that does not belong to us, and we surrender it to Europe." In concluding his testimony Blaine said that if there was any chapter in his life of which he was proud, and of the complete and absolute vindication of which in history he felt sure, it was that

The Pan-Americanism of Blaine

in connection with the policy laid down by the administration of President Garfield with respect to the South American states.[16]

This was not the end of Blaine's diplomatic trials in this quarter. While he was secretary of state in the administration of Benjamin Harrison he had to deal with a serious controversy with Chile. This controversy arose as the result of a fatal attack of certain Chilean citizens on the members of the crew of the U. S. S. *Baltimore*. Hence it is known as the *Baltimore* affair.

The incident had a direct connection with the civil war, which broke out in 1891, between the executive and legislative branches of the government of that republic. By the letter of the Chilean constitution, the government was presidential rather than parliamentary in form; but by long-continued custom—the constitution had been in force since 1833—it had become parliamentary. Cabinets regularly resigned when their measures failed to receive legislative support. Not until the administration of José Manuel Balmaceda, who was elected for the usual five-year term in 1886, was the practice seriously questioned. Balmaceda had an ambitious program of reform which he was at first able to promote in harmony with the legislative branch of the government. In time some of his supporters deserted him and he was confronted with a hostile legislative majority. His cabinets were repeatedly overthrown. His administration was embarrassed by the refusal of the Chilean Congress to pass the necessary appropriation bills. He held that in such case both the constitution and precedent authorized him to extend the budget by decree. This he did on January 1, 1891,[17] whereupon the Congressionalists denounced him as a dictator, ruling in defiance of the constitution. The result was civil war.

The opponents of Balmaceda were able to win over to their cause the principal vessels of the Chilean fleet. They established themselves in the rich nitrate fields of the north, and after seven or eight months of preparation moved against Valparaiso. After desperate fighting the city fell into their hands on August 28, 1891. Feeling that his cause was lost, Balmaceda sought asylum in the Argentine legation and immediately published his resignation. A few days later the revolutionary junta set up a provisional government in Santiago with Admiral Jorge Montt as president. As this government was generally accepted by the Chilean people, it was promptly recognized by foreign powers. But its success was not followed by oblivion of the past. There followed a persecution of Balmacedist leaders, many of whom found refuge in foreign legations or fled to foreign vessels. Balmaceda himself, scorning "vulgar escape," and being unwilling longer to embarrass the Argentine minister by his presence in the legation, committed suicide, in the vain hope that his death might relieve his friends from further punishment.[18] The provisional régime continued a few months longer, when, after an election, Montt was legally installed as president of the republic.

The *Baltimore* affair occurred in the interval between the downfall of Balmaceda and the reëstablishment of constitutional government in Chile. Upon the outbreak of the revolution the United States dispatched to the scene of conflict three naval vessels to protect American interests, one of which was the *Baltimore,* under the command of Captain W. S. Schley. On October 16, 1891, while the *Baltimore* was lying in the harbor of Valparaiso, Captain Schley gave shore leave to one hundred and seventeen petty officers and men of his crew. After they had been ashore a few hours they were attacked, toward six o'clock in the evening, in several localities of the city, by a numerous mob composed of Chilean sailors, longshoremen, and citizens. It was charged that some of the police also joined in the attack. One American was killed, another later died of wounds received in the mêlée, and still others were brutally stabbed and beaten. No Chileans were killed. None even received serious injury, for the Americans were unarmed and defenseless. It does not appear that the shore party had done

The Pan-Americanism of Blaine

anything to provoke so furious an onslaught. The police, who arrived tardily, arrested a number of American sailors, but they were later released; nor did the authorities after a thorough investigation bring any charges against Captain Schley's men.[19] The government at Washington, duly informed of the affair, took the position that this was no mere sailors' brawl to be dealt with by the usual disciplinary measures. It was, according to the American view, a serious and premeditated assault, animated by hostility to the men as American sailors, and hence constituted an offense for which the United States was entitled to demand reparation.

At the time this incident occurred, Blaine was ill at his home in Maine. He did not return to Washington until a week or two later. On October 23, Acting Secretary of State Francis W. Wharton complained in a telegraphic communication to Patrick Egan, the American minister at Santiago, that though a week had passed since "this cruel work" took place, yet no expression of regret or of a purpose to institute proceedings against the guilty parties had been made to the United States. The provisional government gave assurance that the affair was being investigated, but as this was done in a communication offensive in tone, the government at Washington resolved to postpone further discussion of the matter until after the inauguration of the constitutional régime. In his annual message to Congress, however, in December, 1891, President Harrison promised to bring the subject to the attention of that body for such action as might be necessary, if the just expectations of the United States should be disappointed, or if further delay should intervene.[20]

The portion of the President's message referring to the incident, together with a report on the subject by the secretary of the navy, was immediately published in Chile. These publications greatly enraged the Chilean minister of foreign affairs, and he vented his anger in a public letter in which he declared that there was no exactness or sincerity in what was said at

Washington. This insult strained the relations between the two countries almost to the breaking point. For a time Minister Egan suspended intercourse with the Chilean foreign office, and the surveillance to which the legation had for some time been subjected, because of the political refugees harbored there, became at last so intolerable that the Argentine minister, as dean of the diplomatic corps, was moved to protest.[21]

As was expected, the tenseness of the situation was relieved with the change of government in Chile, which occurred late in December, 1891. Events now moved rapidly, though not smoothly, toward a final adjustment of the controversy. The new Chilean minister of foreign relations, Luis Pereira, expressed "very sincere regret for the unfortunate events" which occurred at Valparaiso, and he withdrew, with some qualifications, the offensive language of his predecessor. When Blaine insisted on a full and frank withdrawal, the Chilean government countered by asking for the recall of Minister Egan, on the ground that he was *persona non grata*. These evasions Blaine met with peremptory demands. The President, he said, after giving careful consideration to everything submitted by the Chilean government touching the assault on the crew of the *Baltimore,* was still of the opinion that the attack was directed against the uniform of the United States, and that the public authorities had flagrantly failed in their duty to protect our men. If the demands of the United States were not satisfied, therefore, the only course open would be to terminate diplomatic relations between the two countries. Concerning the recall of Minister Egan, that was a matter which could well await the Chilean reply, as it would then be known whether any correspondence could be maintained with that government upon terms of mutual respect.[22]

Four days later, no response having been received from Chile, the President laid the whole matter before Congress. On the same day the Chilean reply was delivered to Minister Egan at Santiago, but not in time to forestall the President's

The Pan-Americanism of Blaine

message. Signed by the minister of foreign affairs, Pereira, it was an able, statesmanlike document, which at last met the just demands of the United States in a straightforward and dignified manner. After reciting the substance of the American demands, Pereira set forth the views and decisions of his government. He gave assurance that the people of Chile, far from entertaining a feeling of hostility toward the uniform of the United States, had esteemed and respected that uniform ever since the days of the glorious struggle when they saw it figuring honorably in the ranks of the sailors and soldiers who established Chilean independence. He admitted the gravity of the attack on the American sailors, again expressed regret for the occurrence, explained the cause of the delay in arriving at the facts in the case, and extenuated the ineffective action of the Chilean police. He urged that due allowance should be made for the disorganizing effects of the civil war which had just been brought to a close, and in further extenuation he recalled the words of Secretary of State Blaine, in which he contended that as no nation, however civilized, could guarantee its own citizens against violence growing out of individual malice or a sudden popular tumult, the foreign resident must be content in such cases to share the same redress as was offered by law to the citizen.

Nevertheless the Chilean government did not hesitate to condemn, in vigorous terms, the act committed on October 16, or to offer just reparation. For the purpose of determining the reparation due, Pereira suggested that the Supreme Court of the United States or a special tribunal of arbitration be designated. He deplored the employment of the offensive expressions by the former minister of foreign relations, and in fulfillment of a high duty of courtesy and sincerity toward a friendly nation, he declared that they were absolutely withdrawn. This frank and explicit declaration, he hoped, would carry to the mind of President Harrison and of the American people the conviction that the government and people of Chile were moved by a lively desire to maintain unalterable the good and cordial relations which had hitherto existed between the two countries. Finally, with regard to the suggested recall of the American minister at Santiago, Pereira stated that no action would be taken without the accord of the United States.[23]

This note of the Chilean minister brought the dispute to an honorable and happy conclusion. The amount of the reparation was later fixed by direct negotiation at $75,000. This sum Chile paid to the families of the men killed and to those who were injured. Referring to the settlement in his annual message the following December, President Harrison said that the reparation was accepted not only as an indemnity for a wrong done, but also as a most gratifying evidence that the government of Chile rightly appreciated the disposition of the United States to act in a spirit of fairness and friendliness in its intercourse with that brave people. Further evidence of the mutual respect and confidence existing between the two nations was furnished, said Harrison, by the fact that a convention submitting to arbitration the mutual claims of the citizens of the two republics had been agreed upon. Here we may add that that convention was negotiated in Santiago by Patrick Egan. He continued, as long as Harrison was President, to serve the United States as minister to Chile.

In connection with this incident, Blaine was subjected to much unjust criticism. His detractors explained the violent outburst of the Chileans against the American sailors as an expression of resentment due to Blaine's domineering attitude in 1881, and to his interference in the civil war in 1891. Much of the criticism revolved about Patrick Egan. It was charged that he owed his appointment to his influence with the Irish vote; that he was tactless and inexperienced; that he allied himself for personal reasons with the fortunes of Balmaceda, who was trying to suppress democratic institutions and establish a vulgar dictatorship; that because of this corrupt relationship he did not report fully and impartially the course of

The Pan-Americanism of Blaine

events; that he needlessly antagonized the British and Germans in Chile; that he exceeded his authority in harboring political refugees in the legation—such were the strictures of the time. Unfortunately the limitations of space forbid the examination of these charges in detail. This may be said: A careful weighing of the available evidence convinces the present writer that they are based upon misapprehensions and falsehoods. Blaine's conduct throughout was correct. Egan was not inept. He demonstrated unusual ability, and, far from being corrupt, he was singularly upright. Moreover, he was tactful, discreet, and courageous. He quite properly maintained friendly relations with the Balmacedist government as long as it survived, and any resentment which the provisional authorities may have felt toward him for this reason, or because of his offer of asylum to the unfortunate adherents of Balmaceda, was wholly without justification.

Blaine and the First Conference

In the preceding paper of this series will be found a reference to the attempt which Blaine made, during his first administration of the office of secretary of state, to bring about a conference of American nations. Though the scheme was abandoned after his retirement from the State Department, yet the idea survived. Impressed by the advocacy of the former secretary of state and by the warm approbation of some of the Latin American countries, various members of the Senate and House of Representatives introduced resolutions in Congress during the next two or three years proposing more or less extensive plans for Pan-American coöperation. But as the administration of President Arthur frowned upon all these measures, none received the approval of both houses. In the last year of Arthur's presidency, however, Congress, at the suggestion of Secretary of State Frelinghuysen, passed an act authorizing the appointment of a commission to visit Central and South America to collect information and to sound the various governments as to their attitude toward sending representatives to Washington to discuss matters of common interest. In due course the commission made its investigation and submitted reports, recommending a conference to promote commercial intercourse and to prepare a plan of arbitration. The Democratic party, which had in the meantime succeeded to power, looked upon the suggestion with favor. Renewed agitation in Congress resulted finally in the enactment, on May 10, 1888, of a law, which was approved by President Cleveland, authorizing a conference to be held at Washington the following year.[1]

In accordance with the provisions of the act, Secretary of State Bayard dispatched, in July, 1888, a circular letter of invitation to the eighteen Latin American states. He designated

---
[1] Superior figures refer to notes on page 166.

October 2, 1889, as a suitable date for the assembly to convene. Within the next few months favorable replies came from the five Central American republics and from Uruguay and Argentina. After November, 1888, when Harrison was elected to the Presidency, no further acceptances were received until the following spring. The delays for the most part caused no concern; for they were occasioned either by the unwarranted expectation that the new administration would announce a change of plans, or by misunderstandings of slight importance, which could easily be removed. But in the case of three of the republics, Chile, Peru, and Bolivia, silence was ominous; for the serious questions growing out of the War of the Pacific, which still divided these countries, might result, it was feared, in their abstention and, possibly, in the failure of the whole enterprise. Chile, being in possession of the spoils of the war, was reluctant to give other powers an opportunity to open the old questions or to interfere in the pending issues. Peru and Bolivia, on the other hand, though they had everything to gain and nothing to lose by joining in the conference, were unwilling to participate unless Chile was brought, as it were, to the bar of justice. They were waiting to see what their adversary would do. Evidently Chile was the key to the situation.

With perfect propriety, Bayard might have left the solution of the difficulty to his successor; but he preferred to attempt an adjustment before the new administration should come into power. For this purpose he entrusted, in January, 1889, a confidential mission to John G. Walker, secretary of legation at Bogotá.[2] Arriving in Chile some weeks later, Walker was able to confirm, in an interview with the minister of foreign relations, what was already believed; namely, that the real objection of the Chilean government was its unwillingness to submit to arbitration questions growing out of the late war with Peru and Bolivia. Shortly afterward, the American commissioner was so far successful in convincing President Balmaceda that the conference would not interfere in these matters that the

Blaine and the First Conference

president at once announced his acceptance of the invitation.[3] With this obstacle removed, general participation was assured, and all the states, with one exception, signified their intention to send delegates. The exception was Santo Domingo. This little republic had a grievance against the United States. A treaty of arbitration and commercial reciprocity, which had been concluded between the two republics in 1884, had remained during the intervening years without ratification by the United States. In view of this fact, the Dominican government declared in its reply that it was not "at liberty to enter into a new discussion of the subjects already settled by the treaty of 1884."[4]

The Conference assembled on the date agreed upon. Though most of the Latin American countries sent one representative only, there were in all thirty-seven delegates.[5] Ten of these represented the United States. As it was agreed that the voting should be by states, this arrangement established no essential inequality. At the head of the United States delegation was John B. Henderson, with whom was associated the veteran diplomatist, William H. Trescot, and others of less note, including the captains of industry Clement Studebaker and Andrew Carnegie. Among the foreign delegates, Roque Saenz Peña, representing Argentina, was easily one of the most distinguished and influential. Of equal importance was the Mexican, Matías Romero. His perfect command of English, his friendly attitude toward the United States, and his genuine enthusiasm for coöperation among the American countries, together with his unusual ability, made him one of the most valuable members of the Conference. Brazil sent three representatives, among whom Salvador de Mendonça was perhaps the ablest. It is worthy of note that while the Conference was in progress, Brazil accomplished the remarkable feat of converting its form of government, without bloodshed, from monarchy to republic. This revolution was accompanied by no change in the delegation at Washington except the resignation of one of the three members. Other countries, including the lesser as well as the greater, were worthily represented. As a whole, indeed, the personnel was such as to give promise of earnest and thoughtful efforts to achieve results of a lasting and beneficial character.

Profoundly stimulated by the prospect, Blaine welcomed the delegates in a carefully prepared address in which he declared that their presence signified much to the whole of America and might signify far more in the days to come; for, he declared, no conference had ever assembled to consider the welfare of territorial possessions so vast, or to contemplate the possibilities of a future so great and so inspiring. He then indicated in general terms what the assembly might accomplish. It could do much to establish permanent relations of confidence, respect, and friendship between the nations of America. It could show the world a spectacle of eighteen independent powers meeting together on terms of absolute equality, without coercion and without secret understandings. It could proscribe conquest and cultivate an American sympathy as broad as the two continents. It would avoid, he predicted, the errors of conventional diplomacy. It would form no selfish alliance against the older nations from which we are proud to claim inheritance. It would, in fine, seek nothing, propose nothing, endure nothing that was not, in the sense of all the delegates, timely, wise, and peaceful.

These remarks the speaker followed with a concise declaration, which may be regarded as his Pan-American creed. He said:

We believe that we should be drawn together more closely by the highways of the sea, and that at no distant day the railway systems of the north and south will meet upon the isthmus and connect by land routes the political and commercial capitals of all America.

We believe that hearty coöperation, based on hearty confidence, will save all American States from the burdens and evils which have long and cruelly afflicted the older nations of the world.

We believe that a spirit of justice, of common and equal interest between the American States, will leave no room for an artificial balance of power like unto that which has led to wars abroad and drenched Europe in blood.

We believe that friendship, avowed with candor and maintained with good faith, will remove from American States the necessity of guarding boundary lines between themselves with fortifications and military force.

We believe that standing armies, beyond those which are needful for public order and the safety of internal administration, should be unknown on both American continents.

We believe that friendship and not force, the spirit of just law and not the violence of the mob, should be the recognized rule of administration between American nations and in American nations.[6]

At the conclusion of his address, Secretary Blaine invited the delegates to be the guests of the nation on a visit to various parts of the country, in order that they might have the opportunity to observe conditions in the United States, and in order that our people might have "the privilege and pleasure of extending the warm welcome of Americans to Americans." The invitation was accepted. Accordingly, after completing its permanent organization, Blaine being elected as president, the Conference adjourned to reassemble on November 18, thus allowing about six weeks for the excursion. Accompanied by a number of prominent American citizens, the delegates visited the manufacturing centers of New England, then turned westward, going to Buffalo and Niagara Falls, thence to Cleveland, Detroit, Chicago, St. Louis, and other middle-western cities, and finally ended their journey with visits to Pittsburgh, Philadelphia, Baltimore, and New York. In the meantime, plans for the Conference were being elaborated.

When the sessions were renewed, the Conference devoted itself with commendable industry to the achievement of the tasks for which it had been assembled. The work was apportioned among fifteen different committees. The mere enumeration of the subjects with which these bodies had to deal will give some idea of the scope and purpose of the Conference.

They were: customs union, communication on the Atlantic, communication on the Pacific, communication on the Gulf of Mexico and the Caribbean Sea, railway communication, customs regulations, port dues, weights and measures, sanitary regulations, patents and trade marks, extradition, monetary convention, banking, international law, and general welfare.[7]

Within the next three or four months the committees brought in their reports, which were discussed and in most cases unanimously adopted. In two or three instances unanimity was not attained. As it happened, differences arose over matters in which Blaine was most concerned. One of these was the proposed customs union, on which both majority and minority reports were submitted. The majority treated the subject sympathetically, but believed that insuperable constitutional difficulties stood in the way of the establishment of a customs union, if by that term was meant the inclusion of several nations in a single customs territory with reciprocal free trade between the states concerned and with uniform tariff laws for the collection and apportionment of duties on foreign imports among the members. A union of a more restricted sort, limited to reciprocal free trade, without a joint administration of duties on goods of nations not members, they favored in principle, but thought it impracticable on a continental scale. Such a union was an ideal, however, toward which the majority thought the nations of America should work, by the adoption of partial reciprocity treaties, which they regarded as alone feasible at the moment. They made recommendations in accordance with these views.

The report of the minority was brief and to the point. It recommended simply that the proposal of a customs union between the nations of America be rejected.

These reports gave rise to a long and spirited debate, which was led on the side of the minority by Saenz Peña, who, together with one of the Chilean delegates, signed the minority report. On the side of the majority, the argument was sustained mainly by Henderson and Romero, with whom were associated representatives of Brazil, Colombia, Nicaragua, and Venezuela. The Argentine delegate, who forced the issue, presented his views with brilliance and energy. Whoever reads the speeches on both sides will be driven to the conclusion that there was no substantial difference of opinion on the economic questions involved; for the majority and minority were agreed as to the impracticability of a customs union; and against reciprocity, which the majority favored, the leader of the minority could say nothing except that the committee had no authority to report on that subject.[8] Though there were good grounds for this contention, yet Saenz Peña was evidently moved by other and more powerful considerations. His real object seems to have been to contest the leadership of Blaine, with whose Pan-American aims he was not altogether in accord. This does not mean that the Argentine delegate was influenced by personal animosity toward Blaine, or by any unfriendly feeling toward the United States. He was merely acting in harmony with the traditions of his country, for Argentina from the beginning of its independence had pursued what was apparently an extremely individualistic foreign policy. It had declined to follow the lead of Colombia at Panama in 1825, and of other Latin American countries subsequently. It was now loath to recognize the leadership of the United States.

While this debate was going on, Blaine presided over the meetings of the Conference, for which task something more that the skill of the practiced parliamentarian was required. To avoid wounding national susceptibilities, much tact and doubtless an occasional departure from strict parliamentary procedure was necessary. It would have been the height of folly if, for example, he had attempted to thwart the ill-disguised attack of Saenz Peña by the use of the arbitrary power of the presiding officer. An incident which occurred at the close of the debate will illustrate the good sense with which Blaine met the difficult situations which arose.

The report of the majority, when it was finally put to vote, was adopted. Three states, Argentina, Chile, and Bolivia, alone expressed disapproval. Paraguay abstained from voting, and on this ground as well as on the ground that the majority report had made no definite recommendation on the subject of a customs union, Saenz Peña moved that the minority report be voted on. Some discussion followed as to the propriety of taking up the minority report after that of the majority had been adopted. Henderson finally suggested that the correct procedure would be to consider the vote by which the majority report had been approved and to let that of the minority come up as a substitute. Blaine, who was in the chair, entertained a motion to this effect, and the roll call was begun. It was soon interrupted, however, by Henderson, who asked unanimous consent to withdraw the motion, since he had discovered that a majority of the United States delegation was not in harmony with his views. There was objection and the roll call continued, to be again interrupted—this time by Quintana, one of the Argentine delegates, who rose, in a spirit of banter, perhaps, to a question of order. He wished to know whether a delegate could, against the majority of his delegation, make a proposal. "That," said Blaine instantly, "is a point of metaphysics upon which the chair himself declines to rule. The roll call will proceed."[9] Though the motion was defeated by a decisive vote, yet Saenz Peña stood his ground, and again moved a vote on the minority report. The chair entertained the motion and it was put; but it was defeated, the result being now five for and eleven against.

The Argentine Republic, it must be remarked, was not averse to all forms of American accord. It had been eager to assume leadership in a concert of a different sort from that proposed by Bolívar earlier in the century, and it was now no less desirous of pointing a way to the united action of the Latin American states in opposition to the plans of Blaine. At the close of his first speech on the customs union, Saenz Peña seized

Blaine and the First Conference

upon the occasion to suggest vaguely what the nature of that action might be. Affirming his love for America, he declared that he did not lack confidence in, or gratitude toward, Europe. "I do not forget," he said, "that Spain, our mother, is there, contemplating with sincere rejoicings the development of her ancient territory through the energy of a generous and manly people who inherited her blood; that Italy, our friend, is there, and France, our sister, who illuminates with the effigy of a goddess, the harbor of New York. . . . Let the century of America, as the twentieth century is already called, behold our trade with all nations of the earth free, witnessing the noble duel of untrammeled labor, in which it has been truly said God measures the ground, equalizes the weapons and apportions the light. Let America be for mankind."[10]

The epigram "America for mankind" was subsequently adopted as a rallying cry, doubtless to the great satisfaction of Saenz Peña, by those who feared the United States and were engaged in efforts to check its influence in Latin America. Interpreting the simple statement of the Monroe Doctrine, "America for the Americans," as meaning America for the United States, the followers of Saenz Peña haughtily proclaimed the nobler conception—America for all mankind. Ignoring the real significance of the Monroe declaration, they were wont to contrast the broad, humanitarian policy of the Argentine Republic with the narrow, selfish aims of the United States. Yet the Argentine statesman's own aims were somewhat less generous than his sententious phrase seems to indicate. It is significant that in the speech from which I have quoted, none but Latin nationalities were mentioned. Whatever may have been Saenz Peña's ultimate object, his immediate aim was a union of the Latin American republics with the Latin states of Europe as a balance of power against the encroachments of the English-speaking peoples. This he revealed with the greatest frankness in an address which he made some years later in Buenos Aires.

In Westminster Abbey and under the dome of the capitol at Washington, said Saenz Peña, were heard "strange rumors, threats against peoples, conflicts of races." These were signs, he declared, announcing the birth of an idea which would not fail to be carried into execution. In the presence of so great a danger he believed it to be incumbent upon the people of Argentina to cultivate friendly relations with the nations of Spanish America. "Let us respect the sovereignty of all these states," he urged, "and let us found upon them and for their benefit a single society with a common destiny, with a view to the defense of this part of America from dangers common to all.... The masterful audacity of James Blaine, who was undoubtedly more intense than Roosevelt, though less fortunate in the affections of the people, wished to make of America a market, and of the sovereign States, tributaries. The idea, economic in form, was in essence political.... A brilliant and haughty spirit speaks and commands one hemisphere in the name of the other hemisphere; gives orders to Europe in the name of our America; and ends by setting up a chancellory of the New World, without the authority of the rest of the States and without delegation of their powers, since they neither ask protection nor need it."[11]

Argentina and the United States did not work at cross purposes so far as other issues before the Conference were concerned. They generally stood together. A notable example was afforded by their united efforts to secure the adoption of a plan of arbitration. The committee on general welfare, to which the subject had been referred for study, submitted the draft of a treaty which dealt with the matter in thoroughgoing fashion. By the terms of this convention, it was proposed to adopt arbitration as a principle of "American international law," and to make it obligatory in all questions, with the sole exception of those in which the independence of one of the parties might be imperiled. Unfortunately the plan did not meet with unanimous approval. The Chileans feared that their government

Blaine and the First Conference

might be obligated, under its provisions, to reopen the old questions with Peru and Bolivia. Moreover, they were unwilling, they declared, "to entertain the illusion" that conflicts affecting the dignity or honor of a nation should be submitted to the decision of a third party.[12] They accordingly abstained from voting, and on like grounds the Mexican delegation withheld its vote. No argument could budge these recalcitrant representatives from their position. The rest approved the draft without a dissenting voice, after which a resolution was adopted expressing the wish that controversies between American nations and the powers of Europe might be settled in the same friendly manner. Mexico joined in approving this resolution. Chile, however, consistently held aloof.

Thus two of the measures which concerned Blaine most—namely, those looking to the extension of commerce by reciprocity and the promotion of peace by arbitration—were dealt with in a manner which he could hardly have regarded as entirely satisfactory. Another proposal, in which he had scarcely less interest, met with a somewhat better fate, owing to the influence which he himself was able to wield in its favor. This was a resolution, complementary to the proposed arbitration treaty and bound up with it, on the subject of conquest. The form in which the proposal was presented gave rise to an extended and acrimonious debate, in which the United States delegation assumed the attitude of opposition to the views of the Latin American delegates, who favored the resolution. When it became evident that agreement on the proposal as it stood would be impossible, Andrew Carnegie, on one of the few occasions on which he intervened in the debate, secured the floor and moved a recess in order that the committee on general welfare, which had the matter in charge, might come together and attempt to solve the difficulty by consultation. The motion was carried and Blaine retired with the committee. An hour later all vital differences had been removed by a restatement of the resolution. Blaine himself took the floor and moved the new wording as a substitute. Without further debate the resolution was now adopted, Chile alone abstaining.[13]

The resolution recommended to the governments represented in the Conference the adoption of the following declarations:

First: That the principle of conquest shall not, during the continuance of the treaty of arbitration, be recognized as admissible in American public law.

Second: That all cessions of territory made during the continuance of the treaty of arbitration shall be void if made under threats of war or in the presence of an armed force.

Third: Any nation from which such cessions shall be exacted may demand that the validity of the cessions so made shall be submitted to arbitration.

Fourth: Any renunciation of the right of arbitration, made under the conditions named in the second section, shall be null and void.[14]

Not only did Blaine's favorite measures lack unanimous support in the Conference, but they failed to obtain even the partial application which might have been expected. Owing to his efforts, a reciprocity provision was inserted in the McKinley Act of 1890, under which, during the next two or three years, reciprocal trade arrangements were made with a number of countries; but before the scheme was fairly tested, the act was repealed by a hostile Congress. Nor did the plan of arbitration have the desired outcome. The governments whose representatives adopted the treaty failed to give it their approval. The declaration against the acquisition of title by conquest, being an integral part of the arbitral plan, was likewise left without the official sanction of the governments concerned. These failures were more apparent than real. In the sequel the nations of the New World have been prone to adopt the trade policy which Blaine advocated; they have given unmistakable evidence of their predilection for amicable methods of settling international disputes; and they have in various ways expressed their aversion to wars of conquest. On this last point the two

Blaine and the First Conference

greatest powers, appropriately, have been most outspoken. Brazil, in 1891, adopted a constitution containing a provision which declared that the nation in no case should "engage in a war of conquest, directly or indirectly, by itself or in alliance with any other nation";[15] and the United States has been repeatedly committed to the same principle by the public declarations of its Presidents and secretaries of state. It is far from the truth, therefore, to maintain that in these matters the labors of the Conference were futile.

The Conference produced at least one concrete result of great importance. This was the establishment in Washington of a bureau of information as the agent, or permanent secretariat, of the International Union of American Republics. Regarded at the time as a minor achievement, it has developed into a unique and most useful organization. Its cumbersome name was subsequently changed to the Pan American Union. Nonpolitical in character, it aims to develop good understanding, friendly intercourse, commerce, and peace between the American nations. It is controlled by a governing board composed of the secretary of state of the United States and the diplomatic representatives in Washington of the other republics. It is housed in a magnificent building in Washington, the gift of Andrew Carnegie, where the affairs of the Union are administered by a Director General, assisted by a numerous staff of experts. At the laying of the cornerstone of this Pan-American building in 1908, the Brazilian ambassador, Joaquim Nabuco, declared that there had never been a parallel for the sight which that ceremony presented—"that of twenty-one nations of different languages, building together a house for their common deliberations."

The Pan American Union is usually regarded as the only important result of the Conference. There is no justification for so contracted a view. Although the acts of the assembly did not eventuate, except in the one case, in any definite and immediate outcome, yet it is far from the truth to maintain that they were therefore of no importance. Indirect and distant consequences must be taken into account. It is not too much to claim that the Washington assembly was the progenitor of the four similar conferences since held successively at Mexico City, Rio de Janeiro, Buenos Aires, and Santiago de Chile. Each of these assemblies can boast of a modicum of achievement for which the first Conference should have a share of the credit. And the series goes on. Another Pan-American gathering, which bids fair to be more fruitful than all the rest, will take place in Havana, Cuba, in 1928.[16] These conferences no longer find it possible to deal with all the matters which demand coöperative action. A multiplication of agencies has been found necessary. Financial and monetary matters, for example, are now discussed in special conferences, whose resolutions are carried into effect by a permanent High Commission. Questions of law are submitted to an international commission of jurists. Subjects such as commerce, highways, public health, labor, child welfare, science, education, journalism, and other matters of common interest are considered in conferences *ad hoc,* and, when necessary, appropriate machinery is created to promote continuous coöperation in these fields.[17] All this must be taken into consideration in any just appraisal of the first International American Conference.

An Aspect of Isthmian Diplomacy

ONE OF the most remarkable agreements in the history of American diplomacy was embodied in Article XXXV of the treaty concluded at Bogotá between the United States and New Granada on December 12, 1846. By the terms of this agreement the contracting parties formed a species of alliance limited in purpose, ostensibly, to the establishment and maintenance of ways of communication across the Isthmus of Panama. New Granada guaranteed to the government and citizens of the United States "free and open" transit across the isthmus by any mode of communication then existing or thereafter to be constructed; and the United States, as an especial compensation for these and other advantages conceded in the treaty, guaranteed to New Granada "positively and efficaciously . . . the perfect neutrality" not only of the transit route but of the whole isthmian area from its southernmost limits to the Costa Rican border. Likewise the United States guaranteed to New Granada the rights of sovereignty and property which that republic possessed over and in the territory in question.

Historians in the United States have devoted not a little attention to this agreement; but they have been concerned almost exclusively with its bearing on the questions of interoceanic communication that arose subsequent to the conclusion of the treaty. The equally important question of origin has been neglected. On this aspect of the subject the general histories and the monographic studies on isthmian affairs that have appeared in this country since the agreement went into effect are silent. The writings of Polk and Buchanan, two of the high participants, are scarcely more enlightening.[1] Even the correspondence of Benjamin A. Bidlack,[2] who signed the treaty on behalf of the United States, leaves the inquirer un-

---
[1] Superior figures refer to notes on pages 166–168.

certain of the forces that shaped the agreement and of the international pattern into which it fitted.[3] What, then, were the conditions out of which this extraordinary alliance arose?

An earlier treaty has an important bearing on the subject. This was the convention of 1824 between the United States and Colombia, then composed of a union of New Granada with Venezuela and Ecuador. When this union dissolved, some half a dozen years later, by the withdrawal of Venezuela and Ecuador, the treaty by tacit assent remained in force between the United States and New Granada. It was limited in duration to twelve years, counting from the date of the exchange of ratifications. Some time before the date of expiration, discussion arose regarding certain of the stipulations. The chief points at issue were the most-favored-nation principle, embodied in Article II, and the prohibition of discriminating duties, provided for in Article III. New Granada contended that these provisions, though perfectly reciprocal in theory, were unequal and burdensome in practice; for, while they stimulated the already prosperous manufacturing and shipping industries of the stronger nation, they deprived the weaker of the only means within its power of encouraging the initiation and development of like enterprises of its own. The southern republic desired therefore some relaxation in the enforcement of the existing arrangement, or some compensation in a new agreement to take the place of the old. But the United States was inflexibly opposed to any abatement or change. Devoted to the principles involved, it desired to see them more, and not less, widely applied.[4] Agreement was thus impossible and the treaty was allowed to expire.[5]

For a while the negotiations ceased. The American chargé d'affaires, Robert B. McAfee, who had tried so assiduously to obtain a renewal of the treaty, closed the legation and quit the country.[6] The next year, however, a new agent, James Semple, was dispatched to Bogotá with instructions to try once more to reach an agreement. Unfortunately the state of disorder

An Aspect of Isthmian Diplomacy

into which New Granada had fallen, combined with the high tone assumed by Semple in his dealings with the authorities at Bogotá, conspired to defeat these renewed efforts; and, after four years of bickering, Semple returned to the United States with nothing to show but the ill will of the New Granadans.[7] As if to try the effect of a different temperament, Washington next intrusted the mission to the cultivated and affable William M. Blackford. The negotiations were now carried on in an atmosphere of the greatest cordiality. Yet New Granada obstinately held its ground. At last, after two or three years of vain effort, Blackford, in violation of his instructions, made concessions, signed a treaty, and, early in 1845, returned with it to the United States.[8] Thus matters stood when Bidlack, later in the year, succeeded to the mission at Bogotá.

The Blackford treaty was not destined to receive the approval of the Senate;[9] but as it was nominally under consideration, a renewal of the negotiations could not at the moment appropriately be undertaken. Moreover, the authorities at Washington, it appears, had grown weary of the endless discussion.[10] Consequently, Bidlack was sent to his post without the customary instructions and full powers; and the defect had not yet been cured when the treaty of 1846 was signed, though Polk gave the impression in his message of transmittal that Bidlack had acted without authority only in respect to Article XXXV.[11] The record on this point is perfectly clear. It shows that Bidlack had no authority whatever; that he became convinced late in the summer of 1846 that New Granada was at last disposed to meet the terms of the United States; that he then wrote to the Department of State for authority and instructions; that he waited in vain for such authority and instructions until the spring of 1847; and that he then, in due form, confirmed the treaty which he had signed, *sub spe rati*, months before.[12]

In acting without authority, Bidlack did not lay himself open to serious rebuke from his government, for with the exception of Article XXXV his treaty was in strict accord with American views. Described by Polk as "liberal & in all respects satisfactory,"[13] it embraced, among the other stipulations for which the United States had so long and so stubbornly contended, the most-favored-nation principle and the prohibition of discriminating duties; and it admitted none of the objectionable features formerly insisted upon by New Granada. If Bidlack committed any serious diplomatic offense, therefore, it was in relation to Article XXXV. Even so, his offense consisted in reluctantly assenting to the insertion of the innovating article as the price of the treaty, and not in officiously and gratuitously introducing it as a notion of his own.[14] Indeed, Bidlack did little more than assent to any of the provisions of the treaty.

He seemed, it is true, to be of the opinion that he had played an important part in bringing matters to a head. He declared in one of his dispatches, late in November, 1846, that he thought he had prepared the way for the isthmian agreement.[15] The evidence, however, shows that the way had been prepared not by the puny efforts of any individual, but by the inexorable force of events—events that led New Granada to believe that its territorial integrity, and perhaps even its very existence as an independent nation, was at stake. On the isthmian frontier the British were making encroachments which seemed to portend a serious loss of territory in that quarter, including possibly the Isthmus of Panama itself.[16] On the southern horizon still more serious dangers loomed. For years Ecuador, or, more properly speaking, its president, Juan José Flores, had been a source of trouble to New Granada. Recently forced into exile, Flores had gone to Europe, and with British and Spanish aid, and perhaps French and Portuguese support as well, had organized an armed expedition which was now expected momentarily to sail for Ecuador. The restoration of Flores would not have been of itself a source of great concern, but, sustained and encouraged by European powers, it seemed to forbode the sub-

An Aspect of Isthmian Diplomacy

jection of Ecuador and the neighboring republics as well to foreign control.[17] It was in the midst of this state of affairs that New Granada was precipitated into the arms of the United States.

The encroachments on the isthmian shore had been progressing for some time. The motive, in part at least, was the desire of Great Britain to control the routes of isthmian transit in compensation for the westward march of the United States;[18] and they were given a color of justification by the specious claim that since Spain had never occupied or possessed the territory in dispute, the revolutionary governments could not have gained title to it by the right of succession. The first overt act occurred in 1839, when Colonel Alexander Macdonald, superintendent of Belize, raised the British flag over the Bay Islands off the coast of Honduras, notwithstanding the fact that Great Britain had renounced all claim to those islands more than fifty years before. The next step was to revive and make effective the claim once asserted, and likewise renounced, to a right of protection over the Mosquito Indians. In pursuance of this purpose, Colonel Macdonald undertook to eject intruders from the Mosquito territory. Accompanied by the Mosquito king, he proceeded in 1841 to the port of San Juan at the eastern terminus of what was then regarded as the most feasible route for a ship canal, and, going ashore with an armed party, expelled the Nicaraguan forces in command of the place.[19] Setting up a Mosquito administration to take over the affairs of the port, he embarked for the New Granadan village of Bocas del Toro on the Chiriquí Lagoon farther down the coast. Here, however, display of the Mosquito flag, salutes to the Mosquito king, and intimations of a future assertion of Mosquito rights, took the place of forcible ejection.[20] But as these measures—usurpations, expulsions, and warnings—proved inadequate, the British took another and more decisive step; that is, they assumed under a thin disguise the actual administration of affairs on the Mosquito shore.[21]

The New Granadans observed these proceedings with much uneasiness. They were disturbed not only by the fear of further encroachment in the direction of the Isthmus of Panama, but also by the usurpations already effected in the name of the Mosquito king; for they claimed the territory usurped, embracing nearly the whole of the littoral of Costa Rica and Nicaragua, as a part of the national domains. Whether the claim was justified or not, the New Granadan authorities asserted it vigorously and in apparent good faith.[22] Moreover, they tried by every means to convince Great Britain of the justice of their cause. Failing in that, they succumbed to fear and mistrust. In the circumstances, they were disposed to regard mere rumors as facts, and irresponsible proposals as evidence of Britain's evil designs.

An incident which occurred shortly before the treaty negotiations with Bidlack were commenced will serve to illustrate the point. Certain articles supposed to have been written by someone connected with British administration of the Mosquito kingdom and published in the *Albion* of New York, were translated and reproduced in the *Seminario de Cartagena* in its issue of June 14, 1846. The purport of the articles was to suggest that a British protectorate be established over the San Blas Indians, who occupied the territory just east of the Chagres-Panama route, and that a communication through this territory from sea to sea be established under British auspices. Such a proposal in normal times might have passed for what it doubtless was—the unauthorized act of some obscure zealot in the British cause. Coming as it did, however, on the heels of other disturbing events, its effect was to deepen the feeling of apprehension. As nothing, it appeared, could be gained by further parley with England, an appeal to public opinion was resorted to. The preparation of the appeal was entrusted to Pedro Fernández Madrid, who was marked for the task by habits of investigation and a trenchant style. Taking the articles which appeared in the *Seminario de Cartagena* as his point

An Aspect of Isthmian Diplomacy

of departure, Fernández Madrid wrote, during the summer and fall of 1846, the series of articles which have been so justly celebrated as a contribution to the history of the Mosquito question. Widely read in New Granada, the articles served to consolidate the national sentiment against Great Britain, and, furnished to foreign governments, they produced, in some degree no doubt, a like effect abroad.[23]

In the midst of the excitement occasioned by these events, definite news of the Flores intrigue reached Bogotá. Upon his expulsion from Ecuador, Flores had been received with open arms in Spain. There, in the summer of 1846, he laid the foundations of his enterprise. Very soon he extended his preparations to the British Isles, where ships, supplies, and recruits were to be obtained. By the middle of November much progress had been made. Three or four vessels, it appears, had already departed for the rendezvous in Spain.[24] Two steam vessels, the *Neptune* and the *Monarch,* which had been acquired from the General Steam Navigation Company and which were now in the docks of the East India Company being converted into ships of war, were about ready to sail. Another steamer, the *Glenelg,* which was to be used as a transport, was in an equally forward state of preparation. An order for 30,000 muskets, thought to be for the expedition, was being completed at Birmingham. Recruiting, particularly in Ireland, was going on openly and with a success alarming to some of the communities whose sons were enrolling in the enterprise. The principal place of meeting for the officers was the Prince of Wales Club in London, under the very eyes of the British cabinet;[25] and yet, no official notice was taken of these activities, though it was notorious from the start that they were in violation of the Foreign Enlistment Act.

The inertia of the British government resulted in a public outcry which grew in volume as the preparations went forward. Late in October a stream of memorials began to pour into the Foreign Office imploring such action as might be necessary to prevent the departure of the expedition. The first of these petitions to be presented was signed by a group of merchants and other residents of London, headed by the renowned firm of Baring Brothers. Soon there were others. One from the merchants and manufacturers of Manchester urged intervention to protect the common interests of trade and to preserve the "national faith and honor"; another of like tenor came from Liverpool; another was sent in by the Committee of the South American and Mexican Association in the form of a letter signed by the chairman, J. D. Powles; and another, originating in Glasgow, was signed by forty-two firms and prominent residents of that city. This last, one of the strongest of the memorials, recited the facts at length and concluded with the warning that if the expedition were not stopped, the outcome would be fatal alike to British life and to British interests.[26] Yet representations such as these, backed though they were by the most powerful influences in the kingdom, could not alone move the government to act. It required the additional weight of South American opinion—the opinion of New Granada, Ecuador, Peru, Chile, and Buenos Aires—to achieve the desired result.[27]

Though protest finally did its work, Lord Palmerston, the spokesman for the government, yielded to it reluctantly and with bad grace. At first he professed ignorance of anything being done contrary to law.[28] It was for those who had knowledge of the facts to take such action as they might think fit. The government, he asserted, could not prevent British subjects from emigrating, nor interfere with vessels sailing with passengers on board, nor hinder legal commerce in warlike stores. Nevertheless, he moved the Home Office to cause inquiries to be made. Two reports, both dated November 3, were soon in his hands.[29] These reports confirmed the charges as to enlistments and as to the conversion of the steamers into warships. Yet it was not until the end of the month that the vessels at last were seized. On the *Glenelg* were found besides the crew two hun-

An Aspect of Isthmian Diplomacy

dred and fifty young men. The officers in charge of the vessel frankly admitted that all on board had enlisted as soldiers or marines. An inspection of the other vessels left no doubt as to the purpose for which they were intended. Nor did Flores himself deny the purpose for which the expedition had been organized.[30]

The arrest of the vessels was still unknown at Bogotá on December 12, when the treaty was signed. Two days before the signing, Bidlack wrote Buchanan:

I have this morning received a letter from our Consul in *Guayaquil* under date of Nov. 16th stating that Equador and Peru are both in a state of much alarm at the threatened invasion of General Flores under the alledged protection and assistance of the Spanish and English Governments. In connection with these reports, different members of the cabinet of the New Granadian Government have enquired of me whether in my opinion the Government of the United States would adhere to the declared policy of not silently permitting the interference of European Governments to change the Governments of the South American Republics against the wishes of the people of those Republics. . . .

The fact is that the eyes of the government and the people of New Granada seem to be turned towards the United States for protection in this threatened emergency, and I have thought it to be my duty to inform you of the fact.[31]

It is unlikely that the news of the arrest would have had any calming effect even if it had been known in time, for the mistrust of England was now deep seated. The long dispute over Mosquito had matured its fruit. Moreover, the connection between Palmerston and Flores had produced misgivings which could not instantly be removed. This connection seems to have been established at the initiative of Flores. At first, a certain Colonel Richard Wright, afterward chief recruiting officer for the expedition in Ireland, served as the intermediary. A little while later, there was a direct exchange of letters, with Flores averring that his proceedings were innocent and Palmerston declining to express an opinion on the subject. When Wright left to undertake his recruiting duties, Flores designated José

Joaquín Mora, a Spaniard of some note and a former adherent of the independence cause in Spanish America, as the go-between. Mora was to give Palmerston the fullest explanations and to receive such information and counsel as his Lordship might wish to transmit in return. In effect, Mora called at the Foreign Office, had a cordial interview with Palmerston, and then set off to report to Flores.[32] What passed on this and other like occasions during the summer and fall of 1846 is not known. It is impossible therefore to say what degree of innocence or guilt the connection involved.

Manifestly, the balance inclines to the side of guilt; and it inclines more decidedly when the weight of subsequent events is cast into the scales. A few weeks after the seizure of the vessels, Flores was in London seeking as an "old and devoted" friend of Great Britain the return of his property. To this end he wrote a letter to Lord Palmerston stating in pathetic terms the grounds of his petition and beseeching an interview. Palmerston replied, setting a time for the meeting and expressing pleasure at the opportunity of making the acquaintance of "so distinguished a Person"; but he was sorry to say that Her Majesty's government could not interfere with the legal proceedings in which the vessels were involved. Four months later, Palmerston instructed the British consul general at Quito to urge upon the government of Ecuador the propriety and justice of restoring to General Flores the property belonging to him in that republic, which property had been confiscated, Palmerston contended, in violation of an agreement made at the time Flores was forced into exile.[33] After that, nothing appears in the record for more than a year. But the connection between the British minister for foreign affairs and the redoubtable Ecuadorian was not broken.

About the middle of 1848, Flores returned to the New World. After an unsuccessful attempt to establish a residence in Panama, he proceeded to San José de Costa Rica, where he tarried for a while to try his hand at fresh intrigues.[34] Associated

An Aspect of Isthmian Diplomacy

with him in his new undertakings was his former recruiting officer, Colonel Wright, who managed by some means to obtain from Costa Rica the appointment of confidential agent before the government of Jamaica.[35] Here again was a channel of communication with the Foreign Office; and through it there soon passed a proposal for the establishment of a British protectorate over Costa Rica.[36] The plan may have been broached before Flores left England. At any rate, it was favorably considered for a while and then abandoned. But the fertile mind of Flores was soon ready with another scheme: the erection of a monarchy in Mexico and Central America to stop the advance of the barbarians of the North.

Attached to the long letter in which Flores made this proposal is a minute in Palmerston's handwriting. It reads as follows: "Thank him for his friendly Communication and say that I shall always be glad to hear from him and to receive by means of his letters the opinions which so distinguished an American Statesman may from Time to Time form of the Progress of Events in America and of the future Prospects of that interesting Quarter of the globe."[37]

The coming of the Whigs to power in the United States in 1849 produced a striking change in the isthmian situation. The Clayton-Bulwer treaty, soon concluded, lessened the tension at every point. But it brought no good to General Flores. It left him in effect without a job. Lord Palmerston had no further need for his services, and the Costa Ricans, who had obligingly submitted to his intervention in their affairs, were now eager to see him depart.[38] In 1851, he found a doubtful welcome in Peru. Until his death, a dozen years or more later, he was a troublemaker in the southern republics; and as the odor of his foreign, and particularly his British, connection clung to him to the end, his presence was at once a reminder of dangers past and a presage of evils to be feared.

The southern republics, it seems fair to conclude in the light of these later events, were justified in regarding the Flores expedition with the most serious concern. Hitherto they had counted on British opposition to nullify schemes of reconquest such as that of 1846. Now it appeared the policy had been reversed. England was on the side of intervention. The consequences were extraordinary. By electing to meet the aggressions of the United States in the north by aggressions of her own in the south, England presented to the republics in Central and South America what seemed to them to be a choice between two evils: possible return to the colonial status, or possible domination by the Colossus of the North. One of these evils, colonial subjection, all alike had formerly endured, and that one all preferred to shun.[30] New Granada's decision was prompt and conclusive. It lies recorded in Article XXXV.

Toledo's Florida Intrigues

José Alvarez de Toledo came to the United States in September, 1811, in the character of a political refugee. He gave it to be understood that he had been compelled to flee from Spain because of his sympathies with the revolutionary movement then beginning to make itself felt throughout Spanish America. He resided at Philadelphia until the end of 1812, and then proceeded to the southwestern frontier. Entering Texas, he took command of the republican army at San Antonio; but, suffering a disastrous defeat, he escaped to Louisiana. He busied himself in that quarter during the next three years or more with the organization and promotion of divers revolutionary enterprises ostensibly in the Mexican interest. About the middle of 1816, he professed a change of heart, abandoned the independence cause, and in December of that year embarked for Spain, where royal forgiveness and honorable employment awaited his return.

The full story of Toledo's activities on this side of the Atlantic has never been told.[1] A little has been written about his relations with Secretary of State Monroe, and a little more about his connection with some of the border incidents; but apart from these very brief accounts there is nothing in the published records to mark his goings and comings, nor to indicate the objects he pursued. His Florida intrigues illustrate the point. In two instances only has his name been even vaguely associated with the state. It has been said that he gave Monroe, in 1811, secret information regarding the designs of Great Britain on the Floridas;[2] and it has been asserted, without proof or detail, that he was the author, with General Mina, of the plots which culminated in the seizure of Amelia Island.[3] In the first instance, Toledo seems to have had little information to give and no purpose to subserve except perhaps to

---
[1] Superior figures refer to notes on pages 168–172.

gain the good will of Monroe; but in the second, investigation shows, he was in effect the promoter of a vastly complicated intrigue which involved the destiny not only of Florida but of Louisiana, and, indeed, of America as a whole. To be understood, this intrigue must be viewed against the background of Toledo's whole career.

The refugee's conduct in the United States justifies mistrust of all his professions of attachment to the independence cause. He was born in Cuba, but despite that fact was more Spanish than American. His father, an officer in the Spanish navy, and his mother both were born in Spain.[4] He himself was educated in the Peninsula, and on growing to manhood followed his father's example by enlisting in his country's navy, in which he rose to the rank of lieutenant. In the war resulting from the Napoleonic usurpation in 1808, he saw service against the invaders. But his naval career was soon interrupted. In 1810, when the national assembly known as the Cortes of Cádiz was convened on the island of León, he was chosen to represent Santo Domingo in that body. Within a year, the course of his life changed again. He vacated his seat in the Cortes and embarked clandestinely for the United States.

It is important to know, if possible, why Toledo took this step. By his own account, which he set forth in a manifesto published at Philadelphia shortly after his arrival in the United States, he fled to escape the wrath of the very Cortes of which he was a member. He had written, it appears, certain letters to his constituents in the island of Santo Domingo, counseling them to take measures for their own safety and well-being and warning them against trusting too much to the protection of the mother country, dominated as it was by Great Britain. These letters by some untoward circumstance were intercepted after they reached the island. They were sent back to Spain and eventually were transmitted to the Cortes accompanied by charges which had been formulated against the writer. An order for his detention and trial followed. It was because he was

Toledo's Florida Intrigues

fearful of the outcome that Toledo sought safety in a country where, as he expressed it, he would be beyond the reach of despotic power.[5] But it is doubtful whether this account reveals the whole truth.

Is it possible that Toledo left Spain with a definite mission? The distrust of England, to which he gave expression in his speeches in the Cortes[6] as well as in the correspondence with his constituents in Santo Domingo, and the friendly associations which he established with Bonapartist agents and sympathizers upon his arrival in the United States suggest the possibility of a French connection. Indeed the Spanish minister, Onis, who watched with attention the refugee's movements, very soon came to the conclusion—at least so he asserted—that the flight from Spain was a premeditated step in an intrigue of the usurper Bonaparte, the object of which was to deliver the unsuspecting Spanish Americans into the arms of France. But after further observation the Spanish minister came to the very different conclusion—again it must be pointed out that this is what Onis asserted—that Toledo was the instrument of a plot instigated by the American deputies in the Cortes with a view to encouraging the colonies to strike for independence. With this purpose, Onis professed to believe, France and the United States were in active accord.[7]

Of these two views, the latter seems the more plausible; for it is not wholly inconsistent with Toledo's own explanation nor with his actions during the first few months of his stay in the United States. Moreover, this view derives a measure of support from a certain document which Toledo had in his possession at the time of his "repentance" in 1816. This was a commission reputedly signed by the Mexican deputies in the Cortes on July 14, 1811, which empowered Toledo, then about to embark for America, to raise an army and establish a revolutionary government in the Internal Provinces of northern Mexico. But the authenticity of this paper cannot be vouched for. The original was torn to bits by Toledo,[8] and the known copies do not, of course, contain the signatures and other data from a study of which the genuineness of the document might be determined. Nor has it been possible by evidence of any other sort to establish the fact that such a commission was ever issued. Until that is done, Toledo's connection with the Mexican deputies must remain in the realm of doubt.

It may be that none of the explanations accords with the facts of the case. Toledo may have been neither a mere refugee, nor a Bonapartist emissary, nor a representative of the American deputies in the Cortes. He may have been at the beginning what he was at the end: a secret agent of Spain. If that was his rôle, the way he played it does honor alike to his loyalty and to his skill; but it is difficult to believe that his character was so stable or his actions so consistent. He seems, on the contrary, to have had an eye always to the main chance.

Why he chose to establish himself in Philadelphia, where Onis also had his abode, is difficult to explain; for life was made miserable for him there, he claimed, by persecution at the hands of that official. In the course of a few weeks, however, the unhappy exile found a friend. A correspondence which he opened with Secretary of State Monroe resulted in his being invited to come to Washington, at Monroe's expense, for an interview.[9] What passed between the two men when they met late in December, 1811, must be inferred in part from scraps of correspondence and in part from the subsequent course of events. Monroe became convinced, it appears, that Toledo was moved by a desire to defeat England's designs on the Spanish islands and the Floridas, with reference to which he professed to have secret information; and that he aspired, at the same time, to play a part in advancing the general cause of Spanish American independence. Of greater interest perhaps to Monroe was the visitor's apparent willingness to serve the United States in the impending contest for territory on the southern frontier; and an agreement of some sort on that head seems to have been reached.[10]

Toledo's Florida Intrigues

What the agreement was, can be determined only by viewing it in the light of certain contemporary events. Some two weeks before Toledo appeared in Washington, the Mexican agent, José Bernardo Gutiérrez de Lara, who had been sent to the United States in search of aid for his country's faltering revolution, called at the White House to present his case directly to President Madison. The President received him with cordiality and expressed sympathy for his cause, but felt obliged to say that since the United States was at peace with Spain, it could not take sides in the contest. It would be feasible however, the President suggested, to send troops to take possession of Texas as a part of the Louisiana purchase; and he intimated that these troops, once they were established on the Rio Grande, could render valuable assistance to the revolutionists. Rejecting this suggestion as inacceptable, Gutiérrez[11] sought in further discussions, mostly with Monroe, some other basis of coöperation.[12] An understanding, the exact nature of which is a matter of conjecture, seems to have been reached at about the time Toledo was invited to come to Washington. The invasion, it appears, was to be effected not by United States troops flying the American flag, but by a heterogeneous expeditionary force composed of Mexican refugees and of American and other adventurers gathered patriotically under the Mexican flag.

The arrangement with Gutiérrez was doubtless a subject of discussion between Monroe and Toledo; and it may have been understood between them that Toledo was to command the expeditionary force. It does not follow, however, that Gutiérrez was a party to any such understanding, though his presence on the border seems to have been required under the plan agreed upon. Both Gutiérrez and Toledo left Washington early in January, 1812, and both, it appears, were to set out soon afterward for the proposed destination. Toledo returned to Philadelphia, where he received on the order of John Graham, chief clerk of the State Department, the sum of seven hundred dollars, presumably to meet the expenses of the journey.[13] For some reason, however, he delayed his departure for nearly a full year. Gutiérrez, on the other hand, embarked within a few weeks for New Orleans. Upon his arrival there he presented himself to Governor Claiborne, to whom he had a letter of introduction from John Graham. Claiborne in turn introduced him to William Shaler, special agent of the United States to Mexico. After a number of conferences with Claiborne, the Mexican agent and the American agent took passage upstream for Natchitoches on the Red River at no great distance from the frontier.[14] During the next three or four months, the two busied themselves—Gutiérrez openly and Shaler secretly—with the organization of the expeditionary force. In August, 1812, the motley assemblage styling itself the "Republican Army of the North" advanced into Texas under the joint command of Gutiérrez de Lara and Augustus W. Magee, who resigned from the United States Army to join the expedition. Shaler was to follow in the event of success.[15]

Why Toledo lingered in Philadelphia while these things were going on, is a question. The Cuban historian Trelles believes that Toledo's immediate purpose was to embark for Havana to begin a revolutionary movement in the Spanish islands, and that it was only when the plans for this undertaking proved impractical that he looked toward Mexico.[16] This opinion is based in part at least on the fact that Monroe gave Toledo a letter—dated early in January, 1812—to William Shaler, who had gone to Havana in 1810 and was supposed still to be there. But Shaler had written Monroe, under date of November 13, 1811, that he expected soon to depart for New Orleans. That information he repeated in subsequent letters, and on December 11, in point of fact, he sailed for New Orleans. Monroe knew at the time of writing the letter of introduction that Shaler had quit, or was soon to quit, Havana; and he must have known very shortly after that he had arrived at his destination in Louisiana.[17] If, therefore, the letter has any significance, it points to New Orleans as Toledo's immediate objective and to Texas, and not to Cuba, as the scene of his revolutionary activities.

However that may be, Toledo did not turn his face toward the west until December, 1812. He then set out in the company of half a dozen officers, all of whom like himself looked to the achievement of some ambition amid the turbulent scenes then being enacted on Mexican soil. At Pittsburgh, one of the number, Colonel Nathaniel Cogswell, abandoned the party. He had been closely associated with Toledo for some months past, and before setting out had begun to entertain suspicions of Toledo's integrity. He had now come into possession of information that seemed to him to convert suspicion into certainty. He felt it to be his duty, therefore, to warn the leaders of the republican army in Texas, which he was able to do by dispatching a letter by mail ahead of the party.[18]

I now pledge you my honor as a gentleman, and as an officer; and I call God to witness the truth of my assertion, that the object of Mr. Toledo is to play the same game with you as Miranda[19] did in Caraccas. It has been fully ascertained that the people of Old Spain, finding that it would be difficult or impossible to prevent the colonies from aiming at independence, have made arrangements to counter revolutionize, assume the garb of Patriots, and to have all the appearance of being persecuted for their Patriotism, in order to obtain the confidence of the Patriots, and to be entrusted by them in important situations, so that when a favorable opportunity occurs to sacrifice the Patriots and their cause as General Miranda has done. Such a man is Mr. Toledo. I pledge you my life on the issue, for I know it to be a fact. To my certain knowledge Mr. Toledo is in close correspondence with his relation the Marquis of Villa Franca a member of the Spanish Cortes—with the Duke of Infantado, a member of the regency;[20] and with others, the most inveterate foes of the Patriotic cause.... The object is to place himself at the head of the expedition, of which yourself and Magee are now the chiefs. He would then get rid of you and Magee as soon as possible, when he would manage everything in his own way; and as far forth as lay in his power to the utter ruin and subversion of the Patriotic cause. Rely upon what I now tell you. Toledo has not a single particle of Patriotism, his only object is by a great shew of disinterestedness, and affected Patriotism to deceive you, and get himself at the head.

As intended, this letter went in advance of the party to Natchitoches, from which place it was forwarded to its destination.[21] Meanwhile, Toledo and his retinue proceeded at a slower rate down the Ohio and the Mississippi to Natchez. There Toledo found himself the object of further mistrust. At Rapides he was humiliated by arrest and brief detention on the ground that he was a French agent. Rumor preceded him and when he arrived at Natchitoches, in April, 1813, the mistrust had become general. But William Shaler was not among the doubters. Receiving his information from high sources, he was little influenced by mere rumor or by unsubstantiated charges. He did everything in his power, therefore, to make known what he regarded as the correct view of Toledo's mission. He was so successful in allaying the suspicion that Toledo ventured to send his subordinates on to join the army and to go himself as far as Nacogdoches, in eastern Texas, to await developments.[22]

But the conditions were not yet ripe for Toledo's assumption of power. Uninterrupted successes had been the portion of the army since it entered Texas eight or nine months before. Though Magee had died in the midst of the campaign,[23] Gutiérrez was able to carry on as the sole commander with good results. He had just won, with the aid of the American volunteers, a brilliant victory over the royalist army, capturing hundreds of prisoners including the governor of the province, taking a great quantity of arms and military stores, and laying the capital, San Antonio, open to occupation by his troops.[24] Now master of the province, he formed a provisional government with himself at its head. His position at the moment seemed secure. In the circumstances Toledo saw no hope of achieving his aim.[25] Accordingly he retraced his steps to Natchitoches, where he continued, with Shaler's aid, to plot against the leadership of Gutiérrez in the Texan régime.

Toledo's Florida Intrigues 105

Several months were to elapse before Gutiérrez was at last forced to yield. His downfall may be attributed in great part to William Shaler. It was Shaler who encouraged the spirit of discontent among the Americans in the army. It was Shaler who laid the ugly charges against Toledo by facing Cogswell—when he appeared on the scene—and branding him as "a base and treacherous calumniator." It was Shaler who gave countenance at every turn to Toledo's doubtful cause. But Gutiérrez himself must bear his share of the blame. He was his own worst enemy. He weakly permitted a number of the officers captured at San Antonio to be butchered, to the great disgust of the Americans and of many of the Mexicans as well; he did nothing to strengthen his position or to pursue his advantage in the neighboring territory; and he failed miserably in his efforts to organize and administer a government suited to the peculiar needs of the situation.[26] In short, it was incompetence at San Antonio no less than intrigue at Natchitoches that opened the way for Toledo.

The dénouement was astonishingly sudden. On July 24, 1813, Toledo set out from the Trinity in eastern Texas for San Antonio, where he arrived early in August. He immediately assumed command, Gutiérrez retiring to Louisiana. In the meantime, Colonel Arredondo with a royalist force advanced from Laredo and took up a position on the Medina River a few miles from San Antonio. Thereupon Toledo mustered his army, freshly recruited and superior in numbers as well as in warlike equipment, and marched out to meet the foe. On August 18 the two forces clashed and after a sharp fight Toledo's band fled from the field in the greatest disorder.[27] From that day the proud Republican Army of the North ceased to exist. A few of its more fortunate members, among whom was Toledo, succeeded in reaching safety across the Louisiana border. So complete was the victory that the independence movement in Texas was left in a state of paralysis from which it was not to recover for years to come.[28] The hopelessness of further effort in the field was apparent at once to Shaler, and he soon returned to Washington. Toledo retired for a while into Tennessee.

Two weeks before the battle, Cogswell died of a fever at Rapides. If he had lived he would have had the dismal satisfaction of pointing to the disaster as the perfect vindication of his charges; but there the matter would have ended. Nothing could cause the tide of opinion to turn against Toledo. He was strangely immune from attacks on his personal character. The men who were with him on the Medina and who fled with him across the border found no reason to suspect him of double-dealing; Shaler continued to regard him as trustworthy; the Mexican insurgents with whom he was associated afterward in divers enterprises believed him to be devoted to their cause; and with few exceptions the chroniclers of the events in which he played a part have to this day represented him as a man of good faith.[29] But poor Cogswell may have been right and the supporters of Toledo wrong.

It might have made a difference if those who retained their faith in Toledo's integrity despite every suspicious circumstance could have seen a letter that Onis wrote in cipher to his government under date of October 7, 1812, more than two months before Toledo set out for the western frontier.

The ex-deputy of the Cortes Toledo came the day before yesterday to tell me that since his arrival here he has been in direct communication with the Government [of the United States] with a view to fomenting revolution in our Americas, particularly in Mexico: that he acknowledges his inconstancy, that he remembers that Spanish blood flows in his veins, that he anxiously desires his pardon and readmittance to the bosom of the fatherland; but that although he recognizes the generosity of our Government and confidently expects to be treated by it with the benevolence with which a father treats a wayward son, he would not be satisfied with the pardon unless, before obtaining it, he gave proofs of a repentance consecrated by some essential service. He assured me that he believed himself to be in a position to render such a service by virtue of the fact that this Government has agreed that he is to go and take command of a body of two thousand men that have been raised in the Province of New Orleans, to which body another of Mexican insurgents in Texas will be united: that his plan is to concert with one of the chiefs of the Internal Provinces an arrangement by which he would surrender unconditionally the troops under his command along with the twelve thousand rifles and three thousand sabers that have been sent by this Government to the insurgents; and he adds that he is certain of success if he is provided with the funds requisite for carrying the plan into effect.[30]

The sum required, five thousand pesos,[31] presented a difficulty. Onis alleged that he did not have such a sum at his command; besides, he was unwilling to pay before the event. He held out the hope, however, that the reward might be even greater if the promise were kept. To encourage Toledo he offered to advance a modest sum to meet the expenses of travel, and he offered further to dispatch a special messenger to enlist the coöperation of the commandant of the Internal Provinces. But Toledo maintained that money in hand was essential to the success of his plan. Since he could not obtain it, and since he had given up his original idea of leading an army against Spain, there seemed to be no reason for his making the journey to the frontier. He gave Onis to understand, however, that he would consider the matter further and return to report his final decision. But he did not return, and Onis concluded that his only object was to obtain money under the false pretense of loyalty to Spain.[32]

Reverting to the subject in a subsequent dispatch, Onis declared that this opinion had been confirmed. Time had passed and still Toledo had not returned. Instead he had slipped away to Washington to confer with the secretary of state, after which he had set out, with flattering promises from that official, for the western front.[33] Onis cautioned the authorities to be on the lookout. If the traitor attempted to enter the dominions of Spain he could be recognized, said Onis, by the following description: "Toledo is of medium height, light complexion, good figure, well proportioned, and about 36 years of age." But Onis gave the warning in a perfunctory manner; for the revolutionists lacked, in his opinion, the leadership and the resources necessary to achieve success.[34] When the news of the disaster on the Medina reached Washington, he showed no surprise. He forwarded to his government an account of the event which appeared currently in the newspapers. In his accompanying letter he betrayed no sign of exultation over the outcome nor of interest in the part Toledo played in the affair.[35]

After the Texas fiasco, Toledo ceased to be, it seems, in any sense an agent of the State Department. On the surface he was a rebel against Spain, and Onís so characterized him in all his official correspondence, with the government at Madrid as well as with that at Washington. Whether this was his true character or not, Toledo played the part successfully for two or three years longer. For a while he was on the Sabine, inciting the Mexicans to shed their blood in the sacred cause of liberty.[36] In 1814 he went to New Orleans, where he was arrested on a charge of violating the Neutrality Act; but he escaped prosecution because no testimony was brought against him.[37] He took part, it is said, in the famous battle of New Orleans, on the American side.[38] During the next year and a half he was engaged, the evidence abundantly shows,[39] in all manner of enterprises intended, ostensibly at least, to promote the interests of the revolutionists. Yet none of his efforts resulted in the slightest benefit to the cause; indeed, in many cases, they seemed to produce the opposite effect.[40] Was this because Toledo willed it to be so?

Many of his dealings with the insurgents suggest a positive answer to this question; unfortunately, however, the limitations of space do not permit this phase of the subject to be inquired into. It must suffice to direct attention for a moment to the parallel case of a certain Juan Mariano Picornell, who served Toledo as aide-de-camp. Picornell, a Spaniard who had played an obscure part in the revolution in Venezuela, went to Philadelphia in 1812, and was one of the small group of men who accompanied Toledo to the West. Cogswell knew him and thought him even less to be depended upon than Toledo.⁴¹ It was Picornell's function, it appears, to go ahead and prepare the way.⁴² He was in Texas weeks before his chief, and if there were any secret negotiations with the royalist commander, Picornell doubtless conducted them. Like Toledo, he escaped to Louisiana and there continued to play the insurgent rôle; but he threw off the disguise long before his chief.⁴³ As early as February, 1814, he gave up all pretense of insurgency, and, being pardoned by his royal master, was thereafter more successful in frustrating the plans of the revolutionists than he had ever been in promoting them.⁴⁴

The defection of Picornell, to be sure, proves nothing; but it heightens the mistrust with which Toledo's acts must be viewed. The striking parallelism between the two cases is suggestive more of collusion than of coincidence. It is difficult to escape the conjecture, despite all Onis's declarations to the contrary, that both set out from Philadelphia to render some "essential service" to the crown of Spain; and if this be fact, the pardon in both cases was a mere device intended, no doubt, to serve the double purpose of disguising the transaction and of inducing other leaders to follow the example set.

Toledo was less fortunate than Picornell in obtaining the prompt indulgence of the crown. It is vaguely intimated that he, too, applied for pardon in 1814,⁴⁵ upon the return of Ferdinand to the throne; but if the boon was not then granted, it must have been because Toledo had not yet fully rendered the service to which he was committed as the duty of a Spanish agent, or as a sign of the true penitence of a recreant Spanish subject. Be that as it may, his continuance on the frontier put him in possession of a vast amount of information regarding the connivance of American authorities in the efforts of the revolutionists to dismember the Spanish empire in the New World;⁴⁶ and that information presumably would be of great value in consolidating European opinion against so unholy a combination. When, therefore, Toledo quit New Orleans, about the middle of July, 1816, after a final repentance,[47] he did not go, crestfallen and ashamed, to assume the difficult task of rehabilitating a traitor's name: he went buoyantly to lay the fruits of his labors at his master's feet.

But he was not yet to embark for Spain, nor was he immediately to lay aside his Patriot garb. Returning late in the summer of 1816 to his former haunts in the eastern part of the United States, he professed still to be attached to the Mexican cause. He renewed old associations and made constant companions of the numerous revolutionary agents who now congregated in the principal cities of the Atlantic seaboard. With Onis, his relations perforce were secret. Months passed and no one seemed to suspect him. Meanwhile he was busy with his intrigues. In New York he attempted, with false designs, to encourage Joseph Bonaparte to assert his claims to the Mexican throne.[48] In Baltimore he spied on Xavier Mina and succeeded,[49] it appears, in interesting him in a scheme to launch an attack on Florida. Then, accompanied by Pedro Gual, a representative of the revolutionary government of New Granada, he went to Washington to lay the plan before the State Department. Owing to the fortuitous circumstance of Monroe's absence from the city, the visitors conferred with John Graham, who communicated at once the substance of the conversation in writing to his chief. Thus a record of the transaction was preserved.

Genl Toledo and Mr. Gual were with me yesterday [wrote Graham] to say that they had wished to have seen you, to assure you that the Patriots of Mexico & So America would do no act in the Ports of the U States contrary to Law—that they knew what the Law was and would take care not to violate it—that they also wished to apprise you that the want of a convenient Port on the Gulf of Mexico might perhaps induce them to take possession of Pensacola, but if they did so it would be with no view ultimately to keep it as it ought to belong to the U States. They seemed anxious to know how such an act on their part would be viewed by this govt. On that point I could of course say nothing; but I intimated to them as my

Toledo's Florida Intrigues 111

individual opinion that it was an act on which they ought maturely to deliberate as it might be seized on by the British Ministry as a reason for taking measures against them—and perhaps by bringing them so immediately in our neighbourhood lead to consequences which could not be foreseen and might not be agreeable either to us or to them—Should you & the President think it would be injurious to the U States that the Revolutionary Party should take Pensacola—I am of the opinion that an indirect intimation might be given in time to prevent the attempt tho' perhaps in this I am mistaken—[50]

Here seem to be the beginnings of the Amelia Island affair. Vincente Pazos,[51] whose *Exposition* was written shortly after the event, is the sole authority for the assertion that Toledo and Mina originated, in the summer of 1816, the plot which culminated nearly a year later in the seizure of the island by Sir Gregor MacGregor. Graham's letter supports that view; but it does not show what was undoubtedly true, that Mina was to be the instrument for carrying the plan into execution. The silence of all the contemporary documents on this point is strange, though it is not strange that Graham should have been left in ignorance of the fact. The conspirators, as a matter of discretion, no doubt refrained from disclosing their intention to violate the neutrality laws. Moreover, Mina was already under a heavy weight of suspicion. He had arrived a short while before from England with the nucleus of his Mexican expedition—a ship, supplies, and a few officers,—and deserters from his ranks had spread reports of his plans on all sides. Onis complained, but the government did not interfere.[52] A week or so before the conference in Washington, two vessels of the expedition, one the ship acquired in England and the other a schooner hired in the United States, put to sea. On board were arms and ammunition and some two hundred men, most of whom were recruited in the ports of Baltimore and New York. A few weeks later Mina himself sailed on board a brig, also obtained in the United States, and early in October he joined the first contingent at the rendezvous—Port au Prince.[53]

From this port, Pazos asserts, the invasion of Florida was to be carried into effect. Two simultaneous attacks were to be launched, one under Mina and the other under Toledo. But, says Pazos, the damage sustained by some of the vessels in a storm and the defection of Toledo caused Mina to abandon the scheme and sail away to join Aury at Galveston Island. The concomitant circumstances—the arrival of the expedition at Port au Prince, the damage to the vessels, the delay, and finally the departure for Galveston Island—are amply corroborated by Robinson's narrative and by documentary evidence found elsewhere.[54] The principal facts, however, do not meet with a like substantiation. Robinson's account contains no reference to the supposed descent upon Florida, nor to Toledo's connection with the expedition in any capacity. Official communications and other available documents, published and unpublished, are equally silent, unless a single letter of Mina's be admitted as an exception. Writing from Port au Prince to General Montilla, Mina declared that "T—— remained in Philadelphia because of the withdrawal of Gabriel and others."[55] That "T——" was for Toledo is not, in the light of all the circumstances, a rash surmise.

If it be assumed then, as the evidence seems to warrant, that the Pazos account is substantially correct, it is interesting to speculate on the motives of the two protagonists of the enterprise. Mina undoubtedly acted in good faith. Intrigue was foreign to his character. A devotee of liberty, he had been forced to flee his native Spain soon after Ferdinand returned to the throne. He made his way to England, whence he embarked, with British assistance, on his expedition for the liberation of Mexico. The Florida invasion, whether it first occurred to him before his arrival in the United States or after, seems to have been incidental to his main purpose. Disappointment at Port au Prince may have caused him to banish the idea from his mind altogether. If so, he soon had occasion to give the subject fresh consideration; for while he was busy at Galveston Island

Toledo's Florida Intrigues

with his preparations for the invasion of Mexico, he received overtures from certain persons in New Orleans who desired to have him lead an attack on Pensacola and who offered to furnish men and arms for the purpose. Accordingly he went to New Orleans, early in 1817, to investigate the proposal; but finding it to be, in his opinion, a mere mercantile speculation from which no advantage would accrue to his Mexican undertaking, he rejected it. For, "As a soldier and a patriot," says Robinson, "he disliked to war for mercenary considerations, and he was most decidedly hostile to all predatory projects."[56]

The matter may not have been as simple as Robinson makes it appear. It is not improbable that the New Orleans overture was of a piece with the Toledo intrigue. Spanish agents—Picornell and Father Sedella, perhaps—in collusion with Onis may have been attempting to do what Toledo had failed to do; that is, for reasons known to themselves they may have been attempting to divert the Mina expedition from the coast of Mexico. Yet Mina, despite his unwillingness to lead the attack against Pensacola, saw the advantage of an insurgent base in Florida,[57] and he may still have cherished the hope of obtaining one on that coast. In April, 1817, his expedition, escorted by Aury's privateers, landed at the Mexican coast town of Soto la Marina.[58] His purpose was to hold that port, or some other convenient place on the Mexican coast, as a point of contact with the outside world. In any logical development of the plan, Aury's function would have been to acquire an additional port in Florida, and to keep communication open between the two places. There is no proof that such an understanding existed. But in view of all the circumstances—Mina's known interest in the subject, the relations between Mina and Aury, and the raising of the Mexican flag by Aury at Amelia Island a few short months later—the conjecture is not wholly without justification. If the plan was never fully realized, it was perhaps due more to Mina's failure in Mexico than to Aury's mismanagement of affairs at Amelia Island.

Toledo's motives are more difficult to divine. In part, his purpose was no doubt to frustrate Mina's plans.[59] The expedition, it seemed obvious, could not be prevented from sailing, given the weakness of the neutrality laws and the indifferent attitude of the government at Washington.[60] If it landed in Mexico it might do infinite harm, for Mina's prestige and his capacity as a leader might readily turn the balance in favor of the revolutionists. If it could be diverted to Florida, which was doomed to be lost in any case, it would spend its strength in vain. Moreover, the resulting delay would give Toledo or some other agent time to compass its destruction by boring from within.[61]

Yet destruction of the expedition was not the only object sought. The actual seizure of a Florida port was no less desired. That being the case, Pensacola could hardly have been the objective, for its defenses rendered it impregnable against a force such as that at Mina's command. Shortly before Mina sailed from Baltimore, a rumor, probably inspired by the conspirators themselves, that Pensacola was to be seized by the Patriots, was circulated in the public press. During the fall of 1816 and spring of 1817, the rumor gained fresh currency from time to time.[62] Meanwhile, the eyes of the conspirators must have been on defenseless Amelia Island in the other corner of the State. At any rate, there, months later, the blow was to fall.

But why should Toledo, a Spanish agent, instigate an attack upon his own sovereign's territory? The answer to this question has already been intimated: to precipitate a war in which England or another European power, or powers, would be brought to the side of Spain. Shortly before the Toledo intrigue came to a head, Onis wrote his government that the United States had taken measures for strengthening the defenses of West Florida and Louisiana in anticipation of a possible war with Spain. The authorities at Washington desired the war, said Onis, but in order to make it popular they were attempting to maneuver Spain into the position of the aggressor. Beginning with the insult to the Spanish minister in 1809,[63] there

Toledo's Florida Intrigues

had been a long series of acts of offensive to Spain. The Floridas had been invaded, Mobile and Pensacola had been taken, the insurgents had been permitted to operate on our soil, our agents had fomented revolution throughout the Spanish colonies, and privateers had been allowed to fit out in our ports to cruise against Spanish commerce. Behind all these acts was the deliberate intention of provoking Spain to declare war. Dread of complications alone prevented the United States itself from taking the initiative. "The only thing that restrains, or can restrain, this government," declared Onis, "is the fear that England, France or Russia might make common cause with us...."[64]

The United States undoubtedly was restrained by the fear of European intervention; but it was restrained even more by the confident expectation of attaining its end by peaceful means.[65] Spain, on the other hand, had everything to lose unless a general war could be provoked. To the achievement of that aim its agents in the United States seem to have been directing all their efforts. Just before Toledo returned to Philadelphia from the West, Onis proposed in a letter to his government a measure which, if it had been carried into effect, would have resulted inevitably in the desired conflict. His idea was to cede the Floridas—if the United States declined to accept them in exchange for Louisiana—to England or, better, to France. War of course would result, and Louisiana would be recovered and ceded to one of the allies. Spain would perhaps reserve the island and city of New Orleans for itself. Thus, a powerful and ambitious nation whose subversive principles were a menace to the monarchical form of government would be confined to limits within which it could do no harm.[66]

After he had had an opportunity to confer with Toledo, Onis wrote again, adding fresh details. The cession of the Floridas to England, it now appeared, was to be in the nature of a bribe to hold that power in check. Spain itself would take Louisiana. Toledo would see to that. His knowledge of the conditions in the territory and his influential connections there admirably fitted him for rallying the disaffected population to the standard of Spain. The conquest made and a friendly power installed, assistance would always be at hand in time of need. The western states of the American Union, cut off from the navigation of the Mississippi and the other rivers that flow into the Gulf, would eventually be compelled to reunite with Spain. The tranquillity of Mexico and of all the colonies to the south would be assured.[67]

The *Mesa,* a section of the foreign ministry to which these letters were submitted for recommendation, endorsed on the first a brief report which in part reads as follows:

> Onis's idea of ceding the Floridas to England in order to remove the Anglo-Americans from our vicinity would be like chasing a fox out of the sheepfold and throwing in a wolf instead. England has been, is, and will forever be the natural enemy of Spain and of every power that has coasts or colonies, or that may have ships or foreign trade.[68]

The second letter bears a similar indorsement. A man of Onis's talent should have perceived, declares the report, that Toledo was openly mocking him. The talk of conquering Louisiana was ridiculous. It was equally absurd to count upon any assistance from the inhabitants of that territory; for they were the ones who had been most active in giving support to the insurgent cause. That was a strange way to show love for Spain.[69]

These were the views, it must be observed, of underofficials who may not have known that the seemingly fantastic proposals had a practical end to serve; that is, that they were intended to trap the United States into assuming the offensive to ward off imminent attack. If this were the purpose, it was essential that knowledge of the plot should be permitted to leak out. The conspirators, it may be presumed, attended to that detail. In the midst of the affair, Colonel T. S. Jesup, commanding the United States forces in Louisiana, wrote Monroe:

> I have positive information that an attack is contemplated by the Spaniards on this City [New Orleans] during the present season—

The Spanish Minister De Onis, has a number of Agents in this Country, who are, I understand, endeavouring to ascertain what individuals are favourable to Spain, and are using other means, for the purpose of organizing a revolution. The last mail brought a letter from the Minister on the subject. I am not at liberty to say how I obtained my information, but you may rely on the correctness of the fact.[70]

Some two weeks later Jesup wrote:

A secret negociation is going on between the courts of Madrid and London for the purpose of transferring to Great Britain the Floridas and the Island of Cuba, for which, it is understood, she is to assist in reducing to subjection the revolted colonies of Spain. This information is derived from a person in the confidence of the Spanish Consul and who has seen the papers.[71]

Aroused by this information, Jesup was disposed to precipitate the conflict; for he was a strong believer in the offensive defense. It was his intention, at the first hostile gesture on the part of Spain, to occupy Florida; and, with the assistance of the naval commander on the station, he proposed to carry the war deeper into the enemy country by seizing Cuba, the key not only to the islands and the Spanish Main, but to all western America.[72] But there were cooler heads. "If the offensive defense alluded to by this officer," said President Madison, "should be carried into execution it would be perhaps the boldest project ever assumed by no higher authority." Yet the matter was not, as Madison saw it, of trifling importance. He thought the intriguing at New Orleans was probable and the meditated attack possible, though he would have said impossible if there had been less of folly in Spanish councils or less likelihood of foreign support for Spanish undertakings. In any case, if mischief were brewing our minister at Madrid would discover it. In the meantime it would be sufficient to pay attention to such precautionary measures as prudence and the means at our disposal might warrant.[73]

If aggression on the part of the United States had been the outcome, the conspirators might have had their wish. The Old

World might have combined against the New. The conditions on the whole favored such an alignment. The reactionary governments of the continent were strongly inclined to lend assistance to Spain. Feeling toward the United States was generally hostile. "The Royalists everywhere," said J. Q. Adams, who viewed the situation from the vantage point of London, "detest and despise us as Republicans.... Emperors, kings, princes, priests, all the privileged orders, all the establishments, all the votaries of legitimacy eye us with the most rancorous hatred."[74] An obstacle, to be sure, stood in the way of the desired combination. That obstacle was England. This power had steadfastly refused to intervene by force of arms to restore the rebellious colonies to their former subjection. Moreover, its policy was to maintain friendly relations with the United States.[75] Yet popular feeling in England as elsewhere was hostile toward the upstart republic, and the feeling was heartily reciprocated on this side of the Atlantic. In the circumstances a trifling incident might have brought the two powers to blows.

Influences tending to produce the incident were constantly at work. During 1815 rumors of the cession of Florida to Great Britain were repeatedly circulated in the British press.[76] Whatever the purpose, the effect was to exacerbate feeling between the two nations. The rumors were so persistent and so circumstantial in character that Adams went early in February, 1816, under instructions from his government, to make inquiries at the Foreign Office. He was assured that the reports were without foundation. "Military positions," said Lord Castlereagh, "may have been taken by us during the war of places which you had previously taken from Spain, but we never intended to keep them. Do you only observe the same moderation. If we shall find you hereafter pursuing a system of encroachment upon your neighbors, what we might do *defensively* is another consideration."[77] But British troublemakers continued to busy themselves with Florida. The machinations of Colonel Nicolls more than anything else, perhaps, set in motion the train of events that resulted in the execution of Arbuthnot and Ambrister. War on that occasion would have been the outcome, Lord Castlereagh afterward declared to Rush, "if the ministry had but held up a finger."[78]

If Jesup's offensive defense had been undertaken, and especially if it had been directed against Cuba, the finger of the British ministry might have been raised in 1816. But the conspirators must have known that such a move would be made only in response to a warlike gesture on the part of Spain. The Florida intrigue gave promise of throwing the onus of aggression on the United States. By the secret Act of January 15, 1811, the President had been authorized to take possession of Florida in the event of an attempt on the part of any foreign government to occupy it. The act was still in force, and the policy of the administration was still to carry it into effect, if occasion demanded.[79] In the light of these facts, the visit of Toledo and Gual to Washington for the purpose, as they alleged, of apprising the government of their intention to seize a Florida port takes on fresh significance. "They seemed anxious to know," said Graham, "how such an act on their part would be viewed by this govt...." Graham's guarded reply that the contemplated seizure might lead to British intervention or to other consequences disagreeable to the United States must have been encouraging to Toledo, if not to Gual. But more encouraging must have been Monroe's reply to Graham directing that "Mr. Toledo" be told that in the event the revolutionists took possession of Pensacola, the law of 1811 might be considered applicable to the case.[80] How ingenuous was Monroe in all his dealings with Toledo!

With Spanish territory invaded by the United States, the rest would be simple. England would immediately undertake to repel the invasion by force of arms. That this was the view of the agents in the United States can scarcely be doubted. The principals in Madrid entertained a like view, though they may have been unacquainted with the full details of the Florida plot. But principals and agents both were reckoning without their host. A private letter of Castlereagh's to Wellesley, British ambassador at Madrid, written shortly after the events of the summer and fall of 1816, throws a flood of light on the subject.

I think Spain cannot be too cautious in avoiding by every possible means a quarrel with that power [the United States]; and don't let her falsely calculate upon embarking Great Britain in her cause by such an expedient. I make this remark the rather, because I observed in the note presented in October by Fernan Nunez, but which was prepared at Madrid, an assumption that we had pledged ourselves to resist by War any Encroachment on the part of America in the Dominions of Spain.[81]

The assumption, Castlereagh went on to say, was based erroneously on his conversation with Adams—the one alluded to above—the substance of which had by some means become known at Madrid. In concluding this interesting communication, Castlereagh said:

I have stated thus much, in order that you may correct any Misconceptions you find to prevail, & which do mischief in proportion as by holding out false hopes of involving other States in their Quarrels, the Spanish Govt. postpones, from day to day, adopting a rational Course of Policy for itself.

This counsel went unheeded. Spain obstinately pursued its course. It preferred to believe that the great powers of Europe, England included, could be brought to support its cause. It was loath to abandon the position of innocent victim of atrocious wrong. It did nothing to adjust its differences with the United States. On the contrary, it permitted conditions to arise which at last resulted in the courted violation of its territory. Late in 1817, the military and naval forces of the United States took possession of Amelia Island to suppress the establishment formed there some months before by Sir Gregor MacGregor. If Spain itself had destroyed the establishment, which it could have done with slight effort,[82] the United States would have been deprived of its pretext for invading Florida on that occasion. Likewise, Jackson's invasion a few months later to punish

Toledo's Florida Intrigues

the Seminole Indians would have been forestalled if the Spanish authorities had not complacently allowed certain British subjects to embolden the Indians by imbuing them with the false belief that England would come to their support. On neither of these occasions did the desired European interposition result; yet it must be remembered that it was in connection with Jackson's invasion that England and the United States were brought to the verge of war.

These invasions were in some sense the culmination of Toledo's Florida intrigues. When they occurred, however, their author had already embarked for Spain. Before his departure, the break with his insurgent past was made public by what appears to have been a carefully prearranged plan. Toledo, it is known, contemplated sending an agent to Havana in the summer of 1816.[83] The ostensible object was to revolutionize Cuba; but it is perfectly well established that Toledo was not now, if he had ever been, a devotee of the cause. If, therefore, the agent went on the mission, and the evidence shows that he did, his object must have been different from the one assigned. Undoubtedly it had to do with Toledo's exit from the insurgent stage. In November a packet of letters, prepared, it appears, with design, was dispatched by the captain general of Cuba to the Spanish minister in Washington.[84] On the way, also by design, no doubt, these letters were allowed to fall into the hands of insurgent agents, by whom they were delivered to the editor of a newspaper in Baltimore.[85] All except two communications in cipher, which could not be read, were published. Among these published letters was one from Toledo's father to Onis inclosing a bill of exchange for two thousand pesos to be delivered to the son in the event he fulfilled his promise; and another from the father to the son exhorting him to follow the path of honor and give proof of his true devotion to the king.

To his own government, Onis characterized the interception and publication of the letters as an outrageous act, unheard of among civilized nations. He would have complained to the authorities at Washington and brought suit against the publisher, but was advised by eminent counsel that nothing could be accomplished by such a course. In his opinion the worst of it was the probability that all the correspondence of the legation, both going and coming, was tampered with.[86] The reader of the dispatches, indeed, is led to suspect that Onis always acted on this belief; that is, that he committed to the ordinary correspondence only what he was willing to have, or designed to have, any foreign government read, and that he carried on really secret communication by safer means. His complaints about the interception of the letters must therefore be taken with reserve, and likewise the further complaint that the publication of the letters spoiled a plan that he had projected with Toledo for bringing to an end forever the interference of the Americans in the Mexican revolt. The truth of the matter probably is that Toledo's "defection" and departure were in exact accordance with a carefully laid plan.

Toledo's Florida intrigues did not end with his abandonment of American shores. He spent several years at the Spanish court, in evident favor with the cabinet, to whom he gave advice on American affairs.[87] In the summer of 1819, while Spain was searching for some means of evading ratification of the treaty of cession signed at Washington on February 22 of that year, Toledo was sent to London to arrange, if possible, the sale of the province to Great Britain. The plan was for England to advance six million dollars by way of a loan to enable Spain to discharge the American claims and thus get rid of the treaty lately concluded at Washington. The Floridas would then be made over to Great Britain as security for the repayment of the loan.[88] On being informed of the mission by Wellesley, Castlereagh conceived that it might have consisted merely of a report put in circulation to feel the ground, or that it might have been connected with some "low intrigue" of the camarilla at Madrid, or of persons interested in the recent grants of crown lands

Toledo's Florida Intrigues 123

in the Floridas. By taking this view, which he made known to the Spanish ambassador, Castlereagh forestalled all negotiation.[89] Thus the last Florida intrigue with which Toledo was connected came to a fruitless end.

Shaler's Pan-American Scheme

Among the various schemes proposed in the early part of the nineteenth century for the creation of a grand confederation of independent American states, that of William Shaler is in some respects the most interesting.[1] Submitted to Secretary of State Monroe in 1812, shortly after the United States declared war against England, this extraordinary paper was laid away in the archives of the State Department, where it has remained in obscurity to the present time. It was the product of a mind greatly disturbed by the situation then confronting the world. In Europe profound changes were taking place, and it was doubtful what the outcome would be or how the peace and well-being of the rest of the world would be affected. Napoleon seemed invincible. He had marched from victory to victory, humiliating the great states and incorporating the lesser ones in the French Empire. The balance of power, the vital principle of the European system, seemed hopelessly destroyed. England, the only barrier against the universal dominion of France, had usurped the rule of the seas; and Shaler feared that every nation, sooner or later, would be compelled to receive its laws from one or the other of these mighty rivals.

What, in the circumstances, should be the policy of the United States? As our rights were trampled on and our feelings insulted by both England and France, Shaler doubted the wisdom of joining either against the other. But if he had to choose, he preferred England; for the two English-speaking nations, he declared in language that has since become trite, were "destined by Providence to be the guardians of the liberties of mankind." He hoped that our declaration of war would bring England to her senses, that her infatuated ministry would fall, that wiser counsels would prevail, and that the two nations would join in a common effort to insure their mutual safety.

---

[1] Superior figures refer to notes on page 173.

France would then be left in possession of her power, to the benefit, perhaps, of civilization as a whole. A general pacification would result. Spain and Portugal being hopelessly absorbed in the European system, their derelict colonies in the Western Hemisphere would gravitate into the orbit of influence exercised by the United States and Great Britain. These two friendly powers would encourage the people in the different sections of that vast colonial empire to set up governments suited to their peculiar needs; would urge the states thus created to confederate on principles calculated to insure their own happiness and the peace of the world; and finally, would refrain from meddling in the internal affairs of the new states and at the same time engage to protect them against all external interference. The United States and England, in short would form with the proposed confederation a grand alliance of the free nations of the world.

The states of the confederation, Shaler suggested, should be five in number: one to embrace Central America and Mexico another New Granada, Venezuela, and Quito; another Peru another the territory now comprised in the republics of Argentina, Uruguay, Paraguay, Bolivia, and Chile; and finally, one to be erected on the foundations of the Portuguese colony of Brazil. The Spanish possessions not otherwise disposed of would be divided between the protecting powers. To the United States would fall Cuba and the Floridas; to England, Puerto Rico and Santo Domingo. From England the United States would receive Canada and Nova Scotia. By way of compensation, England would take a portion of the territory of Brazil lying along the banks of the Amazon near its mouth; and for good measure she would receive the Philippine Islands as well as other distant possessions of Spain and Portugal. If England objected to any of these transfers, a compromise could no doubt be reached. The United States would not insist on the cession of Nova Scotia, if England felt that the possession of that territory was necessary for the protection of her fisheries.

Shaler's Pan-American Scheme

Likewise, a compromise could be reached in regard to Cuba by setting it up as an independent state; but the annexation of Canada and the Floridas, in the opinion of Shaler, was necessary to the peace and security of this republic.

A certain lack of consistency, it must be observed, characterized these proposals. The contention that the cession of Canada was necessary to the security of the United States had validity only in the event that England continued to be the enemy of the United States. But the very foundation stone of the whole proposal was friendship between these two nations. If that were achieved, security would result without annexation. Still more inconsistent was the failure to observe throughout a proper regard for well-developed national sentiment. The suggestion that England annex a portion of the territory of Brazil is a case in point. Such a transfer would have done violence not only to the sense of nationality already existing in Portuguese America, but to the whole spirit of the scheme as Shaler conceived it. The suggestions with respect to the Floridas and the Islands were less objectionable from this point of view; for nowhere in these areas, with the exception of Haiti, perhaps, had national aspirations found decided expression. As for the rest of the continent, Shaler manifested more consideration and a better understanding. Under happier circumstances the states of his proposed confederation might have come into existence in nearly the form suggested by him. Mexico and Central America later, in fact, were united for a brief period; New Granada, Venezuela, and Quito did combine under Bolívar's leadership to form the Republic of Colombia; and in the southern part of the continent the idea of a single sovereignty, embracing the territory later erected into five separate states, was long entertained. It is not at all likely, however, that a mutilated Brazil would have closed the list with ready acquiescence.

For some reason, Shaler did not propose any exact partition of western North America. He had nothing to say about Texas, to which the United States asserted a claim based on provisions of the treaty for the cession of Louisiana. He made no reference to the country beyond, including New Mexico and California, the possession of which was so soon to be regarded as essential to the fulfillment of our national destiny. He omitted from consideration the northwest coast, where the United States and England faced each other in hostile attitude. Yet he could not have been unmindful of the questions that were sure to arise respecting the ownership of this boundless section of the continent. He had firsthand knowledge of the Pacific Coast, and at the moment of drawing up his proposal the vast western panorama lay, as it were, before his view. Appointed in 1810 as a special agent to Mexico, he had gone, early in 1812, to Natchitoches in western Louisiana to await developments. There the organization of the Gutiérrez-Magee expedition went on under his very eyes, and indeed with his counsel and material assistance. He had seen this band of refugee Mexicans and volunteer Americans invade Texas and, at the time he wrote, expected soon to follow in its wake to San Antonio de Béjar. It must have occurred to Shaler, therefore, that if this venture succeeded, the United States would then be in a much more advantageous position for negotiating with both England and Mexico regarding this western country. Hence his reserve.

In retrospect the scheme may appear fantastic; but viewed in the light of the conditions existing at the time it was conceived, it does not seem altogether absurd. Its ultimate aim was to create a world balance of power to take the place of the disrupted balance of Europe. That was not a strange idea. In those dark days the same thought occurred to Simón Bolívar, and somewhat later—less than a year and a half after Shaler's proposal—the Liberator's views on the subject were set forth in a report of his secretary for foreign affairs. "The ambition of European powers," the report reads in part, "imposes the yoke of slavery upon the other parts of the world, and these all ought to make an effort to establish the balance between themselves

Shaler's Pan-American Scheme

and Europe, with a view to destroy the preponderance of that part of the world. I call this the balance of the world, and it should enter into the calculations of American policy."[2] Bolívar did not at this time, it is true, conceive an elaborate scheme in which the United States and Great Britain would play a prominent part; but later, when Europe was consolidated under the Holy Alliance, his thoughts began to assume a striking resemblance to those of Shaler. The central idea in both cases was the same: United America and England against the world. The difference was in details. In the Liberator's plan, the confederation of new states in greatly elaborated form was to assume the position of leadership assigned to the United States in Shaler's scheme. Moreover, in his later thinking Bolívar went beyond the idea of a union of America and England as a balance against a consolidated Europe: he dreamed of a gradual accretion to the group of free nations, ending in the federation of the world.

The text of Shaler's plan[3] follows.

WILLIAM SHALER'S PROPOSAL

I have ever believed that common justice on the part of England, and a due appreciation of the political importance of the United States would prevent war with them; I am confident that she will severely feel its effects; I believe that the declaration of War by us, will restore her to her senses; and that a ministry such as *may be formed in England* will be desirous of restoring harmony between two states that seem destined by Providence to be the guardians of the liberties of mankind. I therefore humbly submit to the reflections of the wise, the following outlines of a plan for a general pacification. The points it embraces are new, perhaps extravagant, but as hints I flatter myself they may be usefull, and susceptible of great improvement. The present situation of the civilized world is new: History presents us with no semblance of it: latent principles either unknown, or disregarded before, spring up with Vigor and activity, and seem irresistibly to claim the attention of the statesman and the Philosopher.

The political ballance in Europe being irrecoverably destroyed by the humiliation of the great states on the continent, and the incorporation of the minor ones into the French Empire; and the rule of the ocean usurped and maintained by Great Britain; the whole civilized world seems on the point of being forced into a contest against their consent, and against their interests, the object of which seems to be to ascertain from which of the two great powers they may quietly secure laws. It seems impossible according to the immutable laws of nature that the weak must cede to the strong, that the political ballance can again be restored in Europe. The resources and courage of England will struggle in vain against the power of France on the continent; they may for a time retard the catastrophe, but they must finally cede and leave the French Emperor master of the Peninsulae [sic] of Spain. Neither does it seem probable that Russia can oppose any effectual resistance to the overwhelming power of France, and prevent her from organing the turkish Empire and turning its immense resources to the accomplishment of her views of universal dominion. England alone in this old world seems to rise in the majesty of her strength & oppose an insurmountable barrier to the destructive ambition of Napoleon. England alone in the eyes of every reflecting man is the sole dike between him and universal dominion at least in Europe. But England under the controul of an infatuated ministry and an imbecille prince makes an abuse of the advantages of her situation; and instead of being a consolation and a blessing to mankind she violates in the most wanton manner the sovereign rights of other states: the same rights that she pretends to be herself contending for, and renders her influence even more abhorrible than that of France. In this state of things what can be done? what should be the policy of the U.S.? Their rights are trampled on, and their feelings insulted by both England and France: they have allmost equal cause of war with both of those unjust powers. A union with the latter would probably be the ruin of the former, which would leave them in the necessity of subscribing unconditionally to the plans of France, or to engage in war with her single handed. But it appears that if England were governed by wise councils, that a coalition might be formed with the american confederation that would insure the safety of both states, and leave France not only in possession of her power but under it beneficial to the World. As the independence of European Spain is absolutely unattainable, it should be abandoned as such: all treaties having that object in view should be considered as null. There is no dishonor in abandoning an impracticable object, and there are other interests still existing which if properly fostered and managed may again restore the political ballance, and give peace to mankind. The Spanish and Portuguese colonies in america contain an active population of more than twelve millions of souls besides Indians; those countries abound in provisions; timber; every species of raw material; and the precious metals: their soil, climates, sea coasts, bays and harbors, seem to mark them as destined by nature to favor the greatest devellopment of human industry if they were freed from the shackles of barbarism and ignorance, and under the influence of wise and patriotic governments. The Union in friendship of England and the U.S. and consequent action in concert of those two powers would cause discord to cease in those fine countries; would give the people full liberty to chuse and organize such forms of government as best suit their manners, habits, and local circumstances; and finally to unite them in a grand confederation on principles best calculated to insure their own happiness and the peace of the world. This confederation should be formed on principles that remove forever every political jealousy. England may have a fair claim to such indemnities as shall give complete security to her possessions in the East and West Indies; and the U.S. require the same for the security and future peace of the Union. It is therefore presumed that a treaty formed on the fo[llo]wing basis would attain and secure the objects desired. Viz.

Article 1°. The provinces of the Canadas; Nova Scotia; the Island of Cuba; and the Florida's with their respective dependencies shall be forever united to the American Confederation.

Article 2°. A portion of Brasil begining at a convenient boundary south of the river amazons and extending north and west to the southern limits of French Guiana; the Islands of Puerto Rico and Santo Domingo; and the Philipine Islands with their respective dependencies shall be forever united to the British Empire.

Article 3°. The remaining Spanish provinces on the Continent of America shall be united into Sovereign independent States, under such forms of government as their respective inhabitants shall elect, and their independence be forever guarrantied by the contracting parties. Their inhabitants shall be invited to adopt the following political limits as the most natural Viz.

1°. The provinces north and west of the Istmus of Darien to form a sovereign state.

2°. The provinces lying on the atlantic from the Istmus of Darien to the western limits of Dutch Guiana, and on the pacific ocean from the same Istmus to the S. E. limits of the Province of Quito to form a sovereign state.

3°. The remainder of the Provinces forming the Vice Royalty of Peru in their whole extent to form a sovereign state.

4°. The Vice Royalty of Buenos Ayres and the Captaincy General of Chile to form a sovereign state.

The Contracting parties pretend not to meddle with or interfere in the political or civil concerns of the above mentioned states, further than at their request to furnish them with the necessary aid to prevent every foreign power whatever from a similar interference. But they shall be invited to join in a grand confederation for the purpose of securing the great interests embraced in this treaty; and shall not but by common consent make a separate peace with the common enemy during the present War.

Observations on the foregoing Treaty.

1°. As the Canadas must be regarded as at the mercy of the U.S.; as they are necessary to the future peace and security of the Union; and as in the hands of England they will ever be considered as a germ of War, it is believed that no insurmountable objection [to] their cession can be made. Nova Scotia may be a subject of more discussion from the probability of its being regarded as necessary to the prosperity of the British fisheries.

Cuba is certainly of incalculable Value and importance: if it is duly apreciated objections will certainly be made to its union, to obviate which an arrangement may be made for its intire independence, which if properly secured would be as beneficial to the U.S. as its incorporation into the Union. To the cession of the Floridas no objection is foreseen. It may also be observed that the great and important acquisitions that will naturally fall to England in the European and African Seas; such as Cyprus; Candia; Sicily; Sardinia; the Belearic Islands; the Azores; the Canaries &c ought to annull any jealousy she might feel at the acquisitions of power to the U.S. contemplated in this arrangement.

2°. The command of the navigation of the amazons gives England the most complete security for her southern continental possessions, and may also be regarded as a very important source of commercial prosperity. The Islands of Puerto Rico and Santo Domingo, considered as colonies, are of incalculable importance.

The Philipine Islands are necessary to the security of the British Empire in the East: besides their importance as terretorial posses-

Shaler's Pan-American Scheme   133

sions of the greatest value, they will give to G.B. the command of a most important commerce with Mexico, Peru, and Chile. The only objection foreseen to this cession is, that it can be obtained without our consent.

It may be objected that these cessions are made at the expense of the Spanish monarchy, the ally of England, but in reply it may be observed that this arrangement is predicated on the necessary conquest of Spain & Portugal, where those portions of territory however valuable they may be, must be regarded as a derelict: they belong to no one, unless it be to the conqueror of the Peninsulae.

The Continental Spanish provinces have no interest in claiming them, or the means of supporting their claims if they had the interest. The Kingdom of Brasil will be amply remunerated for the inconsiderable cession required for England by the security they will acquire for the vast remains of their territory.

Those provinces which by this arrangement are created into independent states, will undoubtedly be the greatest gainers, as by it they will acquire a powerfull and competent garrantie for their independence, and every obstacle is removed to the formation of regular governments, which if they have common sense, will secure their national prosperity & happiness. Finally this arrangement secures to the U.S. their natural boundaries, and the intire command of the navigation of all their great rivers: and it is believed that it would place the confederate States in intire independence of France and oblige her to conclude a general peace on principles consistent with the future safety and independence of all parties.

Bolívar After a Century

SIMÓN BOLÍVAR breathed his last near Santa Marta in Colombia on December 17, 1830. In February following, the news was published in the press of the United States and Europe.[1] The notices were for the most part perfunctory in character, meager in detail, cautious in the appraisal of the Liberator's achievements, and noncommittal as to his probable place among the historical figures of the world. There was one notable exception. An account which appeared in *Le Temps* (Paris) was unreservedly eulogistic.[2] It began by declaring that America had lost its torch; it proceeded with encomium heaped upon encomium; and it ended with an apostrophe to Bolívar characterizing him as the providence of two hemispheres.

Praise so effusive in the midst of the general apathy is remarkable. Inevitably one's curiosity is aroused as to the authorship of this rare eulogy. It was contributed to *Le Temps*, then a neophyte journal of little repute, by some enthusiast who subscribed the initials "D. P." We do not know with absolute certainty what name those letters represent, but we have good reason to believe that they personate Dominique de Pradt, better known as the Abbé de Pradt. The abbé had been at one time in the good graces of Napoleon. Having fallen into disfavor, he sought a new hero to worship. Bolívar, just then beginning to attract the attention of the world, won the abbé's entire devotion, and the abbé became an ardent champion of both the leader and the cause in numerous publications which issued from his pen for a dozen years or more following the close of the wars in Europe.[3]

These writings, well calculated, as they were, to conciliate European opinion, brought the abbé to the favorable attention of Bolívar. In the course of time a correspondence sprang

---

[1] Superior figures refer to notes on pages 173–174.

up between the two, and the exchanges resulted in the establishment of relations of friendship and mutual admiration. But as the Liberator mounted toward the pinnacle of his fame, his friend and admirer sank into the depths of privation. A letter conveying a well-timed hint of this misfortune elicited a generous response. Bolívar offered the abbé from his private means a substantial pension, and invited him to come and reside in the new land of liberty, where, he said, "one roof shall cover us both."[4] De Pradt declined the proffer of hospitality, but under the spur of necessity accepted the allowance. Accordingly the payments were begun, and they were kept up with more or less regularity until Bolívar's own reduced circumstances and virtual exile, in the last few months before his death, made their continuance impossible.

This arrangement became effective nearly six years before the abbé wrote his eulogy—if it is not too venturesome to assume his authorship. Yet the relationship of principal and agent, as it seems virtually to have been, hardly justifies questioning the motive of either party to the transaction. For whatever the Liberator's ultimate aims may have been, the creation of a favorable opinion abroad was essential to success; and whatever the motives of the abbé may have been, he seems to have served his distinguished patron with genuine zeal. Unhappily, the strange connection was of little avail. The Liberator himself after a while fell on evil days. His own people turned against him, and their changed attitude was reflected in a corresponding change in other countries. When death finally took him from the scene of his humiliation, the plaudits of the world had long since ceased to ring in his ears. He was no longer the man of the hour. Hence the indifferent chronicles of his passing.

In the circumstances, the lone eulogy acquires a pathetic interest. A throng, as it were, stands listless about the Liberator's bier, and none but the faithful servant pronounces words of praise. The calm judgments demanded by the historian do

Bolívar After a Century

not ordinarily flow from such a source. Yet in this case the eulogist succeeds in setting his hero forth in something like the true historical proportions. He goes to the heart of the matter in his treatment of the famous last proclamation, issued by Bolívar from his deathbed six days before the end. The newspapers generally printed this document along with the notices of the Liberator's death. None but the account in *Le Temps* attributed to it any extraordinary significance. It was addressed to Colombians, and as the eulogist interpreted it, its burden was, "Union, union; else devouring anarchy." In Bolívar's thought, according to De Pradt, this counsel embraced Europe as well as Colombia; for, the abbé asserted, the same passions were common to both and threatened both alike with anarchy.

In retrospect, Bolívar's monitory "union or anarchy" seems to have been prophetic, and particularly so if it really was intended to apply to Europe, where the failure to unite has caused so much blood to flow. It should be observed that neither the circumstances of the issuance of the proclamation nor the very words of that document seem to justify so broad an application. Yet the claim, made by a person who had at his command the most intimate sources of information, cannot too lightly be dismissed. It is worth inquiring whether the Liberator did in effect entertain ideas of union so far-reaching. His deeds and his words must resolve the doubt.

The starting point of all his schemes of union was Venezuela, the land of his birth. Long before its independence was achieved, he dreamed of uniting it with New Granada to form a single state. After years of conflict, whose alternating victories and defeats put all the splendid qualities of his leadership to the test, he was able to make the republic of his dreams—Colombia—a reality. But he was not content. Success stimulated his passion for unity. Called to Peru to complete the unfinished task of San Martín, he was again successful, and two new states, Peru and Bolivia, acclaimed him as Liberator. The union of this region with Colombia, that is, the consolidation of the whole extensive territory embraced in the northern and western part of South America from the Orinoco to the confines of Chile and Argentina, now became an object which he pursued with unremitting energy. Unfortunately, it was beyond his power to accomplish the undertaking. Worse still, in the attempt, he caused Colombia to be so shaken that it broke into impotent fragments. Thus he liberated half a continent, but failed to create a nation.

The failure was tragic, for national unity was the very cornerstone of an imposing structure of international unity which for a long time had been taking shape in the Liberator's restless brain. Yet, despite failure, these larger plans are of the greatest interest. They measure the amplitude of Bolívar's outlook and the depth of his understanding. They reflect the processes of his imaginative, feverishly active mind. They attest thoughts that habitually projected themselves beyond the bounds of province, state, and continent into the broader realms of universal concern. They reveal noble purposes. They inspire to fresh endeavor.

At the age of thirty, when as yet he had won no permanent foothold in the territory which he was afterward to liberate, Bolívar was thinking in terms of two hemispheres. It was then, a decade before Monroe's declaration and more than a dozen years before Canning's famous boast, that the Liberator proposed a world balance of power. His idea was that since the European nations aspired to hold in subjection the other parts of the earth, all these ought to unite to establish an equilibrium between themselves and Europe, and thus destroy the preponderance of that part of the world. He was thinking primarily of America and he recommended that the proposal should enter into the calculations of American policy.[5]

Such a balance was, of course, impractical. The idea was transient, for the conditions that suggested it were transient. When Bolívar proposed it, all Europe was at war and no powerful friend of American freedom could be seen in that direction. A little later the complexion of affairs had changed. The wars were ended, and though the Holy Alliance presented a new danger, England seemed to offer a countervailing hope of security. None saw the situation more clearly than Bolívar and none was more eager than he to take advantage of it. He was a genuine admirer of the British constitution and a constant advocate of its use as a model in the political organization of the new American states. He believed that the might of the British Empire, its desire to play a still more influential part in world affairs, its relative freedom from entanglement in the European system, and the sympathetic interest of its government and people in the cause of freedom were considerations which would induce it to take its stand with the free nations of America against the reactionary powers of Europe. To this conception of the balance he held fast until near the end of his career.

Until independence was assured, his immediate aims were national rather than international. What he expected first of all from an alliance with the British was assistance in prosecuting the lagging patriot cause. So adverse had been the fortunes of war that he himself had fled from Venezuela, in 1815, and sought safety under the British flag in Jamaica. The future looked dark. As he was without hope of being able to triumph unaided, he appealed to England for help. He held out as an inducement the political advantages that would accrue to the empire from the resulting world balance. As an additional attraction, he offered to throw Panama and Nicaragua into the bargain, suggesting that the control of the interoceanic canal routes would confirm Britain's dominion over trade.[*] Though the proposed alliance did not meet with official approval in London, it must be presumed that it was not too harshly regarded in that quarter. At all events, when Bolívar renewed the struggle, he was able to carry it to a successful conclusion by means, in great part, of the assistance which came to him unhindered from the British Isles.

As the end of the contest with Spain approached, plans of international scope assumed first place in the Liberator's thoughts. He turned from war to peace. The hope of an alliance with Great Britain endured. Shortly before he undertook to complete the unfinished task of San Martín in Peru, he wrote buoyantly to Sucre: "England . . . desires to form a league with all the free peoples of America and Europe against the Holy Alliance for the purpose of putting herself at their head and ruling the world."[7] Nearly a decade before, he had expressed the devout wish that the representatives of the states of America might some day meet at Panama to deliberate on the high interests of peace and war among themselves on the one hand and between them and the rest of the globe on the other. Military success at last made it possible for him to take steps to realize his wish. Invitations were extended to the American states, and England was urged to send a representative. The inclusion of Great Britain with a view to the establishment of the larger unity in which that power would play the leading part does not signify that Bolívar had abandoned his earlier idea of a lesser unity of American states. Continental solidarity was still one of his aims. But his grand design was a united America in a league of all the free nations of the earth. The achievement of this design was the object of the Panama Congress.

The congress was doomed to failure. The times were inauspicious both in the New World and the Old. In the one, national confusion and international jealousies inhibited action; in the other, policy and calculation forbade participation. Yet despite the unfavorable auguries, Bolívar persevered. Indeed the difficulties seem to have had the effect of enlarging his vision and of strengthening his resolution. In one last effort to win England over to his scheme, he jotted down in a memorandum intended for British eyes a concise statement of the benefits to be obtained from the formation of a league of all the free nations of the earth.[8]

The benefits were these: The American states in their relations with one another would be governed by law; internal order would be maintained; security against external aggression would be assured; equality would be realized; differences of origin and color would lose their influence and power; social reform, in short, would be attained under the blessed auspices of liberty and peace. England's influence in Europe would progressively increase; her decisions would be like those of destiny; her commerce would possess a new domain; her relations with Asia would be facilitated; her subjects would be put on a basis of equality with American citizens; her character and her customs would be taken by Americans as their standard of life; and at last, perhaps, one nation would cover the earth—the federal nation. There was but one indispensable requisite: "England must necessarily take in her hands the beam of the scales."

This memorandum—it was written in February, 1826, and remained unpublished for ninety years—marks the culmination of Bolívar's political thinking. He had gone a long way since the occasion, more than a dozen years before, when he had thrown out tentatively the proposal of a balance between the European and the non-European nations of the world. He had gone a long way from his first conception of an Anglo-American balance against continental Europe. He had gone beyond the very idea of the balance of power. He had attained an ideal that few men have dared to cherish—the federation of the world.

Bolívar's voice was not heeded. The old order with its perilous European balance persisted. The most stupendous of catastrophies was the result. Convinced—at what a terrible cost!—that like periodical disturbances must be the inevitable consequence of such a system, the nations of the world are now more inclined to seek salvation in unity and coöperation.⁹ They have taken a momentous step in the creation of the league which has its seat at Geneva. But the league is weak and much remains to be done. Great areas lie outside the union. Political systems divide the earth. The lesser unities, from which the greater must gain its strength, are yet to be created or perfected. Europe still falters between union and anarchy. The countries that owe their freedom to Bolívar linger indifferent to his counsel of union. Elsewhere in the New World national unity is yet to be attained. The international unity of the American states is still a pious wish. America does not play its full part in the unification of the world.

What can America do to promote world unity? It can first of all effect its own unification. Fortunately, no insuperable obstacles lie in the path. Bolívar, the torch, pointed the way more than a hundred years ago. His light has not gone out. It shines more and more resplendently as the years go by. It is the symbol of American unity. It is a point about which the nations of America can rally. Let them rally. Let them achieve Bolívar's ideal. Let them provide a model for the other great regions of the earth. Let these emulate the American example. Let Europe federate. Let the other regional unities be established. Then perhaps the world can unite. If that day comes, it may not be too much to call Bolívar the providence of the two hemispheres.

Pan-Americanism and Imperialism

Pan-americanism and imperialism appear to be mutually exclusive. Whether they are so in effect is a matter of definition. Neither term in current usage conveys a precise meaning. Pan-Americanism fails because it has not yet emerged into a distinct and easily recognizable form, and imperialism because it has evolved in the course of history through a variety of forms from which a doubtful choice must be made. In the one case the problem is to decide what meaning, and in the other, which meaning. The "what" is the more difficult to determine, since new concepts such as Pan-Americanism acquire meaning with time and circumstance. It is not strange, therefore, that the attempts at formal definition have thus far proved unsatisfactory. Not even the genus to which Pan-Americanism belongs has been agreed upon. One author calls it an advocacy, another an idea, another a sentiment, and still others an aspiration, a tendency, or a doctrine. Obviously it does not fall indifferently into all these categories. If it is a sentiment merely, it is less than a doctrine; if it is a doctrine, it is more than a tendency; and to call it a tendency is not the same as to say it is an aspiration or an idea.

The concept, it may be, is not susceptible of exact classification. One other suggestion, however, is worthy of consideration. Twenty-odd years ago, Secretary of State Robert Lansing called Pan-Americanism a policy—an international policy of the Americas. Implicit in this view is the assumption of an agency of continental scope capable of formulating and promoting the policy. The assumption may have been of doubtful validity at the time Lansing made his statement, but today that objection does not hold. The international American conferences, however ineffective their early efforts may have been, now undoubtedly formulate policy. They do more. They create the machinery for carrying the policy into effect.

If, then, the existence of a Pan-American policy be admitted, does it follow that the concept policy is the genus of which we are in search? Apparently not, for the policy of the Americas is an effect behind which lies Pan-Americanism as the cause. That is, Pan-Americanism is anterior to, and more inclusive than, any definitely charted course, or declared principles, or established organs for common action. It is a force productive of policy, not policy itself. The only way to understand the nature of this intangible force is to observe its concrete manifestations in policy. It will be convenient, therefore, to employ the term policy as if it were in very essence the genus of Pan-Americanism.

What is this policy of the Americas? It is a course of action adopted by the independent states of the New World with a view to the establishment of continental unity on the basis of certain recognized principles which may be stated briefly as follows: the independence and equality of the American nations; community of political ideals;[1] nonintervention; the settlement of inter-American disputes by amicable means; no conquest; and coöperation to achieve the common aim. These principles are deeply rooted in continental thought. Leading statesmen of both Americas have repeatedly asserted them, and the international conferences have confirmed them by numerous declaratory acts. International in scope, the policy rests on national foundations; that is, it rests on the individual policies of the states comprising the Pan-American group. Thus it is the individual policy of each to promote the general policy of all.

The principles of the policy express, it is true, the ideals and not the invariable practices of the American nations. If the ideals and the practices are too much at variance, Pan-Americanism may become a mockery. This is particularly true if the practice of the United States, the most powerful of the nations concerned, is inconsistent with the ideal. It is essential, there-

[1] Superior figures refer to notes on page 174.

Pan-Americanism and Imperialism

fore, to inquire whether this greatest of the American nations does in fact respect the independence and equality of its neighbors, whether it refrains from intervention in their affairs, whether it is disposed to settle its disputes with them without recourse to force, whether it abstains from conquest at their expense, and whether it genuinely coöperates with them to achieve common aims. In short, it is essential to know whether the United States, while professing respect for the individuality and well-being of its neighbors, in reality seeks to dominate them for its own selfish ends—whether it pursues the course of Pan-Americanism or that of imperialism.

The real course is one of imperialism, say some observers. Precisely what these observers mean is not clear, for they do not define imperialism. What does the term signify? Its meaning must be sought in empire. Without empire, actual or intended, there can be no imperialism. If the empire already exists, there must be measures for maintaining it; if it does not yet exist, there must be measures for creating it. The measures for maintaining or for creating empire constitute policy—the policy of imperialism. Thus two policies appear: the policy of Pan-Americanism, and the policy of imperialism. The one is expressly intended to create and maintain a community of equal, coöperating nations; and the other is intended, presumably, to create and maintain an empire. The two policies, the two courses of action, lead in quite different directions. In which of these directions does the United States move? It cannot move in both at one and the same time. It cannot serve two masters.

If the policy of the United States is to create or maintain an empire, what is the nature of this empire? What is the nature of empires in general? History furnishes many examples. They fall into two classes: first, states with vast accretions of heterogeneous outlying areas; and second, more compact states whose chief ruler happens to bear the title of emperor. Of this second class the New World provides some examples in the empires of Dessalines and Christophe in Haiti, of the Pedros in Brazil, and of Iturbide and Maximilian in Mexico. Possessing no dependent territories, these empires, so called, were in no external respect different from the other American states that existed contemporaneously with them. The very title of emperor by its historical associations has acquired a connotation of excessive and arbitrary power. Hence the use of the term imperialism as an antonym of democratic or constitutional government. For example, the departure from strictly constitutional procedure in the United States during and immediately after the Civil War has sometimes been characterized as imperialism. The fashion of the day is to describe this phenomenon as dictatorship. The imperialism with which we are concerned is not of this sort. It seems to derive from the empires of the expansive type.

Empires of this description have flourished in every age of recorded history. Those that exist today are vaster and more powerful than any that have gone before. Of all modern empires the Roman is the prototype. Its essential characteristics were three: first, the central Roman state exercising the *imperium;* second, the outlying conquered territories—Spain, Gaul, Britain, Asia Minor, etc.; and third, control over these areas through the agency of Roman governors and Roman armies. It is worth noting that the early expansion of Rome by the progressive conquest of neighboring peoples until the greater part of Italy was united under one central authority did not constitute empire. This was the process of creating a national state, if we may use the modern terminology. It should be observed also that the larger Roman conquests were of peoples, and not of thinly settled or vacant lands. Nor did the Romans migrate to any considerable extent into the conquered outlying areas. That process, if it is controlled by the parent state, is colonization and not imperialism. Respect for the great historical example from which the very term empire is derived requires that these facts be remembered.

Pan-Americanism and Imperialism 147

The empires of the sixteenth and seventeenth centuries—if the interesting examples of the Middle Ages may be passed over—were of a somewhat different type. They are usually described as colonial. Yet, in two important respects they follow exactly the Roman pattern. First, the parent states achieved the requisite unity and strength to exercise the *imperium;* and secondly, they acquired, as did Rome, distant territorial possessions. In respect to the most notable of the characteristics of the Roman Empire—the control over alien peoples—the resemblance in most cases was not striking. Portugal, for example, devoted itself primarily to trade and colonization. It did not rule over teeming millions in the Far East nor in Africa. In those quarters it was content to dominate small areas about the trading stations to which its vessels resorted for their precious cargoes; and in Brazil it directed its activities not to the government of native races, but to the establishment of its own people and its own culture in a new environment. England and The Netherlands followed much the same procedure. In the Orient they entered into competition with the Portuguese for commercial supremacy, and elsewhere they preferred trade and colonization to the conquest and rule of native races. Both, however, were to establish in the course of time empires of the Roman type.

France established in the seventeenth century an empire much like those of England and The Netherlands. Spain alone approximated the Roman model. Though it was not indifferent to trade and colonization, it made veritable conquests. Mexico, Guatemala, New Granada, Peru, and the Philippines were as truly the provinces of Spain as Gaul or Spain itself ever were of Rome. Nor is the similarity confined to conquest and control. It extends to the common survival of the conquered peoples and to the lasting impress left upon them by the dominant powers. Obviously, imperialism of this sort is different from the movements that resulted in the transference of peoples and institutions to a Massachusetts, a Virginia, a Quebec, a Buenos Aires, or a Cape Colony. Yet the Roman element in the overseas activities of Portugal and The Netherlands and of England and France was sufficient to justify the use of the term "empire" to describe the composite structure erected by each in its sphere of action.

The empires created in the sixteenth and seventeenth centuries suffered a great decline in the eighteenth and nineteenth centuries. In their place new and more powerful empires have risen. The most recent, officially declared less than two years ago, is not only like the Roman, it is Roman. Rome today is the seat of the *imperium* as it was in the time of the Caesars, and the recent conquests have followed with remarkable fidelity the pattern set by the ancient predecessor. About the meaning of imperialism deduced from this example there can be no doubt. And so it is with most of the other existing empires. The Netherlands, building on the foundations laid in the seventeenth century, succeeded in the nineteenth in bringing the Dutch East Indies under its complete domination. It is an empire in the Roman sense. France, with its millions of subjects spread over enormous areas in Africa and Asia, is likewise a true empire. Belgium is another example. The population of its African domain is greater than that of Belgium itself and the area is nearly eighty times as great. Nor is this disparity exceptional. It is characteristic of all present-day empires, as it was of the Roman model.

The British Empire cannot be characterized with like simplicity. From its exceedingly complex structure no precise notion of British imperialism can be drawn. The relation of the United Kingdom to the different parts varies as the parts themselves vary. To the self-governing Dominions the relation is one thing; to India it is another; to the other Asiatic possessions it is another; to the Caribbean colonies it is another; and to the African dependencies it is still another. In respect to the first of these relationships, imperialism does not apply. An essential element is lacking. There is no subordination be-

Pan-Americanism and Imperialism

tween the United Kingdom and the self-governing Dominions. This group of states is, as it has happily chosen to call itself, a commonwealth of nations. We must search elsewhere for British imperialism. It exists in divers forms in the relation of the United Kingdom to the vast aggregate of dependent states and territories. In India, it appears to be developing in the direction of less and less subordination; in the West Indies, it remains of the seventeenth-century colonial type; and, in Africa, where native races are subject to British rule, it is more nearly of the Roman pattern.

We may now inquire into the nature of the alleged imperialism of the United States. Some writers maintain that it dates back even to the first English settlement on American shores. Since imperialism is a policy, it could hardly have existed before a nation capable of formulating and directing the policy came into existence. Was the United States from the beginning of its independent existence an empire? It had, to be sure, territory lying beyond the bounds of the constituent members of the Union, but that territory was wholly unlike the outlying areas of true empires, since it was marked from the beginning for admission into the Union on a basis of equality. Nor did the presence of a relatively small Indian population give it the character of an imperial domain. Many of these Indians, it may be admitted, were unwilling subjects of the United States. To reason from that to empire leads to confusion. On this basis every national state becomes an empire, for all national states in the course of their development have been compelled to incorporate to greater or less degree recalcitrant elements of the population. We must conclude, therefore, that the United States in the early years of its independence was not, under any proper definition of the term, an empire.

Even so, perhaps the policy of the United States was from the beginning to create an empire. Witness the additions of territory at the earliest opportunity. Did not the annexation of Louisiana and the Floridas make of this nation an empire? Not if our definition of empire is valid. Louisiana and the Floridas possessed at the time they were purchased a sparse population, a goodly portion of which was already American. These areas were contiguous and they were more intimately related to the United States than imperial provinces ever are related to the dominant power. Given the territorial form of government and then erected into states, the new acquisitions were in the end fully incorporated into the Union. That was a process of national growth, a process of expansion, not of imperialism. So it was with the subsequent annexations. Nowhere was there any considerable alien population. Texas, with a population predominantly American, took its equal station among the older states; California was admitted with little delay; and the rest of the ceded territory was marked for ultimate statehood.

To inject the question of ethics serves only to confuse the issue. Let it be admitted that the conduct of the United States in respect to some or all of the annexations was not above reproach. Does it follow that the reprobated acts were imperialistic? Wrong may be done in the interest of national growth as well as in the interest of imperial growth. It does not conduce to clear thinking to make imperialism do duty as an opprobrious epithet. Imperialism is a question of fact and not of ethics; and likewise expansion is a question of fact and not of ethics. Here the purpose is not to assess right and wrong, but to determine whether the United States is, or ever has been, an empire. Certainly it had not become an empire as the result of these vast acquisitions. Nor did the United States pursue its policy of expansion with a view to the creation of an empire at some future time. It had the choice between nationalism and imperialism. It is well known that at the close of the Mexican War there was some sentiment, in the United States and in Mexico as well, for the annexation of the whole of Mexico.[2] If that idea had been carried into effect, the United States would have been converted at once into an empire, for it would have had under its rule several millions of alien people. All the

Pan-Americanism and Imperialism

conditions of empire would have been fulfilled. The choice, and it seems to have been a deliberate choice, was against the creation of such an empire.

The dozen years immediately following the Mexican War were characterized by the strange obsession known as "manifest destiny." Yet the exuberance of that period resulted in no further expansion. Nor did the terrible years of civil war permit of any additions to the national domain. The experience of the conflict demonstrated, however, the desirability of naval outposts, particularly in the North Pacific and in the West Indies. To meet the need in the Pacific, Secretary of State Seward revived an earlier scheme for the annexation of Alaska. Successful in achieving his purpose in that quarter, he turned his attention to the Caribbean, where an opportunity seemed to offer in an apparent desire on the part of the Dominican Republic for annexation to the United States. The negotiations which Seward initiated to effect this end were continued in the administration of President Grant. Though the President himself lent the proposal the weight of his fame and the prestige of his high office, he could not induce the Senate to give its approval. The Senate may have been moved in some degree by partisan rancor. It was moved more powerfully, no doubt, by its belief that the Dominican government's proffered annexation did not represent the real desires of the Dominican people, toward whom the duty of the United States, as Charles Sumner phrased it, was as plain as the Ten Commandments.[3] Sumner and his colleagues in the Senate feared, moreover, that one annexation would lead to another; that, in effect, the Dominican annexation would be the first step in the creation of an empire. Like objections did not hold in respect to Alaska; it was then a trackless waste.

To some minds the Spanish-American War in its objects and results provides indisputable evidence of American imperialism. It provides, in fact, the most convincing proof to the contrary. The United States had in 1898 a magnificent opportunity to lay the foundations of an empire, if it had so desired. Spain's possessions in the New World and in the Far East fell into the hands of the armed forces of the United States without difficulty. A considerable body of opinion, both lay and official, desired to have the government embark frankly upon an imperialistic career; but the idea did not prevail. From the beginning, Congress committed itself as far as Cuba was concerned by declaring that the people of that island "are, and of right ought to be, free and independent." It was expected by some observers abroad and perhaps by the imperialists at home that a way would be found to evade the obligation implicit in that declaration. The imposition of the Platt Amendment as a condition precedent to the withdrawal of the American troops may have left the impression that the evasion had been accomplished. Cuba, despite the restrictions, took its place in the family circle of nations, where the subordinate parts of an empire are not welcome. Moreover, the Platt Amendment, proving to be a constant source of friction, has been abrogated;[4] and if anything more needs to be done to prove that the United States really desires that Cuba shall be in the fullest sense free and independent, that too, no doubt, will be done.

The Philippines present an analogous case. No declaration of policy, it is true, accompanied our seizure of those islands, but when such a declaration was finally made, in the Jones Act of 1916, it was couched in these terms: " . . . It is, as it has always been, the purpose of the people of the United States to withdraw their sovereignty over the Philippine Islands and to recognize their independence as soon as a stable government can be established therein."[5] That declaration of purpose is now in process of fulfillment under another act of Congress, passed in 1934. Ten years after the date of this act, the sovereignty of the United States over the Philippines will come to an end. Whatever may have been the aims of some of our statesmen or the hopes of some of our people, the sum total of our relations with those distant islands denies rather than affirms imperialism.

Puerto Rico, like the Philippines, was ceded to the United States at the close of the Spanish-American War; unlike the Philippines, it has never been given the promise of independence. Though its area is not great, its population is more than a million and a half. Here, then, on a small scale, are the apparent conditions of empire; that is, an outlying territory inhabited, indeed saturated, by a population whose language, culture, and institutions are different from those of the dominant country. Yet in area and population Puerto Rico is insignificant compared with the United States. If a swallow does not make a summer, neither does one small island make an empire. Alaska and the Hawaiian Islands cannot be added to it to swell its amount, for they are Americanized areas already seeking admission as states. If the other American islands in the Caribbean and the Pacific be added, there still is no empire in the proper sense of the word. These lesser islands are not even way stations to empire. They are outposts of national defense. Puerto Rico is different. If it is unhappy under its present relation to the United States, that relation will in the course of time be changed to one satisfactory to the Puerto Ricans. A people who deeply believe, as the people of the United States believe, that governments derive their just powers from the consent of the governed will see to that.

The asserters of imperialism contend, however, that the empire of the United States is not confined to definitely annexed areas. It embraces vastly more, they say. They enumerate: the Dominican Republic with such and such an area, so much population, so much trade; Haiti with such and such an area, so much population, so much trade; Nicaragua with such and such an area, so much population, so much trade; and so on the Caribbean round. These, they assert, are within the imperial domain. Add them to all the other dependencies, big and little, from Alaska to Wake Island, and from Liberia to Samoa. The result will be a very respectable empire. So it would be if the areas involved were really under the imperial sway of the United States. Alaska and some of the others that figure in the addition clearly are not imperial territories. Furthermore, the Caribbean republics, the enumerators themselves admit, are not genuine dependencies: they are only "virtual" or "nominal" dependencies. To this, then, the empire of the United States is reduced: one or two real dependencies, little ones at that, and an indeterminate number of the so-called virtual dependencies.

It remains to inquire why certain of the Caribbean republics are designated by some observers as parts of an empire of the United States. The explanation can be expressed in a single word: intervention. Not that these observers are content to characterize the interference by using a word so clearly defined in public law; not that they are willing to withhold judgment as to its results; not that they accept any official declaration as to its ultimate purpose. They assume the object to be empire and point to the armed forces as the proof of empire. Withdrawal makes no difference. If the Marines are brought home today, they will be sent back tomorrow. Empire, like Time, marches on. With it march the ghostly auxiliaries "virtual" protectorate and "nominal" dependency. It is all very confusing.

For this state of affairs the government of the United States must take its share of the blame. The repeated interventions have aroused doubts on the one hand and fears on the other. That is not strange in a world where like proceedings have usually marked the course of empire. It is not strange that observers at home and abroad should fail to discern beneath the surface a purpose as different from empire as day is from night—a purpose of assisting the weak to assume their proper station in the concert of the New World, and not a purpose of merging their sovereignty in that of the United States. Whatever the purpose, the performance has been bad. The interventions have been productive of more harm than good. Moreover, they have contravened the Pan-American rule and the historic policy of the United States as well. Of all this, the government

Pan-Americanism and Imperialism

and people of the United States seem now to be well convinced. If interference in the internal affairs of our neighbors is not yet entirely at an end, it is undoubtedly in the process of coming to an end.

The accusers have, however, another leg to stand on. It is economic imperialism. Here also is encountered extreme indefiniteness of meaning. How does this new imperialism differ from the historic kind? A close analysis may well leave one in doubt. According to some authorities, the three essential elements are present: that is, the dominant state, the outlying areas, and control by the dominant state. The only difference appears to be in the underlying motives, or in the process of acquiring or exercising dominion. These are only differences in detail, the end being annexation as in the old imperialism. According to another view, the concept is more conveniently vague. The *imperium* is a capitalistic combination of vast connections and international reach; the outlying areas embrace the whole field of trade and investment; and the control is a manifestation of power as sinister, as mysterious, and as relentless as the source from which it emanates. This fanciful view of economic imperialism need not detain us. It is enough to say that it is set forth as an attack not primarily on imperialism but on capitalism. The purpose of this paper is not to discuss Pan-Americanism in relation to capitalism. Its purpose is to discuss Pan-Americanism in relation to imperialism, and to that subject it must be confined.

Despite difficulties and doubts, the search for the economic imperialism of the United States must be pursued. Like political imperialism, this kind of imperialism can only be understood in relation to empire. If there is an economic empire of the United States, it must exist somewhere; it must have bounds; it must be open to view; and it must be subject to control, else it is no empire. The asserters of economic imperialism should be able to throw light on this point. If they be asked to do so, however, they are likely to revert first of all to the Marines and to virtual or nominal dependencies. If it be maintained that this is the old and not the new, the rejoinder is economic motive: bankers, loans, concessions, and the like. If it is objected that whatever the motive, the empire described is still political, and if evidence of economic empire pure and simple be demanded, the reply is likely to be more or less as follows: "Behold the billions of dollars of loans to the Hispanic American countries, the oil interests in Mexico, the copper interests in Chile and Peru, the sugar interests in Cuba, the banana industry in Central America, banks in numberless cities, and trade to correspond."

Despite this formidable array, the asserters of economic imperialism do not contend that the whole Hispanic area is the economic province of the United States. They will readily admit some exceptions, and if they are pressed they will admit more. These admissions leave the bounds of the empire very uncertain. This is disconcerting. It is impossible to detect the symbols of possession in a domain whose limits are unknown; and it is equally impossible to distinguish the agencies of control. Whoever insists on being shown some part of this economic province where the symbols of possession and the agencies of control are clearly in evidence will be taken back to the Caribbean; again the political empire. If, in despair of finding the marks of purely economic imperialism in the outlying area, one turns to the United States in search of the central directing authority, the result will be the same. The international combination, which will be suggested as the directing force, is unconvincing. Neither Wall Street nor any other national economic agency seems to gather into its hands the threads of supreme economic control. The national government fails to meet the requirements. Despite innuendo, it does not, it seems, exercise the *imperium* in the interest of the varied and conflicting economic forces. If it does pretend to that function, it fails miserably. The economic province over which it is thought to have control sprawls in disorder, buying and sell-

Pan-Americanism and Imperialism

ing freely, paying and defaulting at will, taxing without fear, and performing every other economic act without the slightest regard for its supposititious master.

To contend that the United States is free from imperialism is not to contend that it is free from the evils often associated with imperialism. The evils exist without empire, and doubtless empire can exist with few of the evils. The use of imperialism, especially where none exists, as a catch-all for everything hateful, leads to muddled thinking. In international relations, as in every other relation of life, terms ought to be employed as far as may be with scientific accuracy. If, for example, wrongs arise from intervention, intervention and not imperialism should be made to bear the blame. If absentee ownership is at the bottom of some economic ill, to talk of economic imperialism will not set matters right. If American capitalists employ unethical means to achieve their ends, it will do no good to stigmatize imperialism. If the strength of the United States overrides the just cause of a weaker state, the false cry of imperialism will bring no redress of the grievance. So in numberless instances the mind is diverted from the real to an imaginary ill. Cure, if that is the object, would be more likely to follow correct diagnosis.

Unfortunately, to alarm the victim is quite as often the purpose. Across the Atlantic, certain interests look with concern on the steady trend toward New World unity. They seem to see in American solidarity an obstacle to the attainment of their peculiar aims—aims which look to the reaping of a material advantage, to the accomplishment of a national ambition, to the imposition of a political system, or to the inculcation of a social philosophy. These non-American interests know that a contented, unfrightened, stable, unified America is not likely to look to them for social panaceas, for economic security, or for political protection. Hence their cry of imperialism. Hence their constant warnings to the weaker countries of this hemisphere against the dangers that surround them; hence their repeated assertions that the real aim of the United States is empire; hence the fiction, endlessly iterated, that Pan-Americanism is a mask of imperialism.

These alarms are not taken too seriously, either in the United States or in the other countries concerned. Foreign influences, it is well understood, will not determine the fate of Pan-Americanism. The New World states themselves will determine that. They will decide whether mistrust, or self-aggrandizement, or petty jealousies shall stand in the way. They will decide—indeed they have decided—that there shall exist on this continent a union of equal, freely coöperating nations. Consequently, they are not deterred by the arguments of those who attempt to prove that the ideal neither has been realized nor can be realized. They know that the differences in language, culture, and racial characteristics, which are sometimes urged as obstacles, are not incompatible with international unity. They know that Pan-Americanism imposes no economic or other restraint on the free exercise of national sovereignty. They know that the fears, suspicions, and hatreds that are supposed to actuate some of the states in their relations with some of the other states do not obscure the larger aims. They know that in Pan-Americanism lie the hopes of a continent.

That Pan-Americanism was the choice of the United States rather than imperialism, is a fact of great moment to the independent states of this hemisphere, and it may prove ultimately to be of vast significance to the world at large. If imperialism had been the choice, the map of the continent would have taken on a different appearance. The republics within the reach of the United States would have been absorbed, while those at a distance would have been driven to seek safety in foreign alliances. America would have become the meeting place of empires. Its vital principle would have become the balance of power and not a concert of nations; its frontiers would have been fortified; its vast area would have been overrun by alien armies; and its peace would have been disturbed by wars of alien origin. Happily, the peoples of this continent do not confront any such situation. Secure under their separate flags, they are free to demonstrate to the world that nations can live together as good neighbors.

NOTES

THE MEANING OF PAN-AMERICANISM

[1] In the issue of March 5, 1888. The New York *Sun* employed the word for the first time September 12, 1889; the London *Times*, September 30, 1889; *L'Economiste Français*, December 28, 1889; and the London *Spectator*, January 29, 1890. The Oxford Dictionary erroneously attributes the first use of the adjective, Pan-American, to the New York *Evening Post* of September 27, 1882. In fact the *Post* admitted the word to its columns exactly three months earlier, that is, on June 27, 1882.

[2] John Bassett Moore, *A Digest of International Law* (Washington, 1906), I, 62.

[3] Elihu Root, *Latin America and the United States* (Cambridge, Mass., 1917), p. 10.

[4] *Collected Papers* (Cambridge, Eng., 1914), p. 92.

[5] *Principles of International Law* (6th ed.), pp. 123, 132.

[6] Quoted by Lawrence, *ibid.*, p. 282.

[7] *Foreign Relations of the United States, 1895*, p. 558.

[8] Westlake, *International Law* (2d ed.), I, 323; Oppenheim, *International Law* (4th ed.), I, 253.

[9] Hyde, *International Law*, I, 28.

[10] By the treaty between the United States and Cuba of May 29, 1934.

[11] *International American Conference* (1889–1890), IV, 40–42.

[12] *Foreign Relations, 1915*, p. xi.

[13] *The Public Papers and Addresses of Franklin D. Roosevelt* (5 vols.; New York, 1938), V, 8.

[14] *Messages and Papers of the Presidents*, James D. Richardson, ed., II, 340.

[15] *International American Conference* (1889–1890), IV, 114.

[16] VI, 23.

[17] P. A. Martin, *Latin America and the War* (Baltimore, 1925), p. 58.

[18] *International American Conference* (1906), Report of the Delegates of the United States, p. 57.

[19] *Bulletin of the Pan American Union*, Vol. XXVI, Pt. II, pp. xx–xxi (May, 1908).

[20] Root, *op. cit.*, p. 63.

[21] Martin, *op. cit.*, p. 372.

[22] *Ibid.*, pp. 363, 570.

[23] Root, *op. cit.*, p. 95.

[24] For good brief accounts of the Tacna-Arica question see *Am. Jour. Internat. Law*, XVII, 82–89, and XXIII, 605–610.

[25] *Am. Jour. Internat. Law*, XXX, 14.

[26] Sumner Welles, "The New Era of Pan-American Relations," *Foreign Affairs*, XV, 445–448.

DIPLOMATIC FUTILITY

[1] J. Q. Adams, *Memoirs* (12 vols.; Philadelphia, 1874–1877), VI, 325–326.
[2] Department of State, Despatches to Consuls, II, 315.
[3] J. Q. Adams, *Memoirs*, VI, 325.
[4] Beaufort Watts to Adams, July 22, 1824, Department of State, Despatches, Central America, I.
[5] Department of State, Instructions, X, 285.
[6] Frederick C. Baker to Clay, September 10, 1825, Department of State, Despatches, Central America, I.
[7] Williams to Clay, March 10, 1826, April 10, 1826, May 6, 1826, August 3, 1826, November 24, 1826, December 1, 1826, January 6, 1827, Department of State, Despatches, Central America, I.
[8] Department of State, Instructions, XI, 258.
[9] Rochester to Clay, May 12, 1827, Department of State, Despatches, Central America, I.
[10] Rochester to Clay, June 3, 1827, *ibid*.
[11] Clay to Rochester, October 7, 1828, acknowledges the divers letters on which the account given above is based.
[12] *The Autobiography of Martin Van Buren*, John C. Fitzpatrick, ed. (Washington, 1920), p. 162.
[13] VII, 399.
[14] VII, 477.
[15] VIII, 42.
[16] VIII, 52.
[17] Livingston to Jeffers, July 30, 1831, Department of State, Instructions, XIV, 209–217.
[18] November 19, 1831.
[19] Henry Savage to Livingston, July 23, 1832, Department of State, Despatches from Consuls, Guatemala, I. See also Charles Shannon to Livingston, August 22, 1832, Despatches, Central America, I.
[20] DeWitt to Livingston, April 15, 1833, Department of State, Despatches, Central America, I.
[21] Livingston to DeWitt, April 20, 1833, Department of State, Instructions, XIV, 315.
[22] DeWitt to Livingston, April 15, 1833, April 30, 1833; DeWitt to McLane, July 2, 1833, August 26, 1833, September 9, 1833, October 20, 1833, November 21, 1833, December 16, 1833, Department of State, Despatches, Central America, I.
[23] DeWitt to Forsyth, November 7, 1835, December 18, 1835, March 29, 1836, October 14, 1836, January 26, 1837, and numerous other letters, Department of State, Despatches, Central America, II.
[24] Forsyth to DeWitt, April 14, 1839.
[25] Jno. J. Bedient to Forsyth, April 16, 1839, Department of State, Misc.
[26] John L. Stephens, *Incidents of Travel in Central America, Chiapas and Yucatan* (2 vols.; New York, 1841), I, 22.
[27] *Ibid.*, p. 39.
[28] *Ibid.*, pp. 41–44.
[29] *Ibid.*, p. 191, *et passim*.
[30] *Incidents of Travel in Yucatan* (2 vols.; New York, 1843).

Notes

[31] The instructions to Murphy are found in Department of State, American States, Instructions, XV, and the letters from him in Despatches, Central America, II.

[32] Kennedy to Aberdeen, July 29, 1844, *British Diplomatic Correspondence concerning the Republic of Texas*, E. D. Adams, ed. (Austin, Texas, [1918?]), pp. 350–352.

[33] Buchanan to Hise, June 3, 1848. These instructions have been published in *The Works of James Buchanan*, John Bassett Moore, ed. (12 vols.; Philadelphia, 1908–1911), VIII, 81.

[34] Hise to Buchanan, October 26, 1848, Department of State, Despatches, Guatemala, I.

[35] December 20, 1848, *ibid.*

[36] May 25, 1849, *ibid.*

[37] Hise to minister of foreign affairs of Nicaragua, January 12, 1849, copy in Department of State, Despatches, Guatemala, I.

[38] Yet the treaty stood for a time in the background as a threat. Cf. Crampton to Palmerston, October 1, 1849, F.O., 5/501.

THE PAN-AMERICANISM OF BLAINE

[1] James G. Blaine, *Twenty Years of Congress* (2 vols.; Norwich, Conn., 1884–1886), I, 572; II, 484.

[2] J. V. Lastarria, *Obras completas* (9 vols.; Santiago de Chile, 1906–1909), V, 373.

[3] James G. Blaine, *Political Discussions* (Norwich, Conn., 1887), p. 411.

[4] Blaine to Morgan, June 16, 1881, *Foreign Relations of the United States, 1881*, p. 768.

[5] Blaine to Morgan, November 28, 1881, *Foreign Relations, 1881*, p. 815.

[6] See *Bulletin of the American Geographical Society*, Vol. XXIX (1897), Nos. 2 and 3, for articles by Matías Romero on the Mexico-Guatemala boundary question.

[7] Diego Barros Arana, *Histoire de la guerre du Pacifique* (2 vols.; 1881–1882), I, 15.

[8] Osborn to Evarts, April 3, 1879, *Foreign Relations, 1879*, p. 160.

[9] Blaine to Christiancy, May 9, 1881, *Foreign Relations, 1881*, p. 909.

[10] Diego Barros Arana, *op. cit.*, II, 112; Osborn to Evarts, March 5, 1880, Department of State, MSS.

[11] Blaine to Hurlbut, June 15, 1881, *Foreign Relations, 1881*, p. 914; Blaine to Kilpatrick, June 15, 1881, *ibid.*, p. 131.

[12] Blaine to Trescot, November 30, 1881, *ibid.*, p. 142.

[13] Trescot to Blaine, January 27, 1882, *Foreign Relations, 1882*, p. 63.

[14] Frelinghuysen to Trescot, January 9, 1882, *ibid.*, p. 58.

[15] *Chile-Peruvian Investigation*, H. R. 1790, p. 21.

[16] *Ibid.*, pp. 217, 353.

[17] Cf. Proclamation of President Balmaceda, *Foreign Relations, 1882*, p. 94.

[18] Balmaceda to Uriburu, September 19, 1891, *ibid.*, p. 165.

[19] Schley to H. Tracy, Ex. Doc. 91, 52d Cong., 1st Sess., p. 293.

[20] *Messages and Papers of the Presidents*, James D. Richardson, ed., IX, 186.

[21] *Foreign Relations, 1891*, p. 273.

[22] Blaine to Egan, January 21, 1891, *ibid.*, pp. 307–308.

[23] Egan to Blaine, January 25, 1891, *ibid.*, pp. 309–312.

BLAINE AND THE FIRST CONFERENCE

[1] *International American Conference* (1889–1890), I, 7.
[2] Bayard to Walker, January 18, 1889, Department of State, Instructions, Argentine Republic, XVI, 463.
[3] Walker to Blaine, No. 1, April 5, 1889, Department of State, Despatches, Argentine Republic, XXVII.
[4] *International American Conference* (1889–1890), I, 26.
[5] *Ibid.*, pp. 49–54.
[6] *Ibid.*, pp. 39–42.
[7] *Ibid.*, p. 61.
[8] For the debates on this subject see *International American Conference* (1889–1890), I, 103–264.
[9] *Ibid.*, p. 259.
[10] *Ibid.*, p. 131.
[11] Roque Saenz Peña, *Escritos y discursos* (2 vols.; Buenos Aires, 1914–1915), I, 162.
[12] *International American Conference* (1889–1890), II, 978.
[13] *Ibid.*, p. 1145.
[14] *Ibid.*, p. 1147.
[15] José Ignacio, Rodríguez, *American Constitutions* (2 vols.; Washington, 1906–1907), I, 166.
[16] The Conference was held as projected. Five years later, another convened at Montevideo, and in 1938 still another met in Lima, Peru. The Peace Conference held at Buenos Aires in 1936 was not one of the regular series of International American Conferences.
[17] From 1826 to the present time more than one hundred such special conferences have been held. For chronological and classified lists see State Department Publication No. 499, Conference Series, No. 16.

AN ASPECT OF ISTHMIAN DIPLOMACY

[1] *The Diary of James K. Polk,* Milo Milton Quaife, ed. (4 vols.; Chicago, 1910); *The Works of James Buchanan,* John Bassett Moore, ed. (12 vols.; Philadelphia, 1908–1911).
[2] Recently made public in *Diplomatic Correspondence of the United States: Inter-American Affairs,* William R. Manning, ed. (Washington, 1935), Vol. V.
[3] The historians of Colombia have done better. Antonio José Uribe, editor of the *Anales diplomáticos ... de Colombia* (6 vols.; Bogotá, 1901–1920), has provided much valuable documentary material bearing on the subject; Raimundo Rivas, in his *Relaciones internationales entre Colombia y los Estados Unidos* (Bogotá, 1915) and his *Escritos de Don Pedro Fernández Madrid* (Bogotá, 1932), supplies much additional information derived from the archives at Bogotá; and other Colombian writers, such as Eduardo Posadas in his *Vida de Herrán* (Bogotá, 1903), and Diego Mendoza in his *El canal interoceánico* (Bogotá, 1930), supplement or confirm Uribe and Rivas. But none of these writers has made any extensive use of the British Public Record Office, and it is to that source that one must recur to complete the story.
[4] Rivas, *Relaciones,* pp. 75–83; Mendoza, *El canal interoceánico,* pp. 88–102;

Notes

Forsyth to McAfee, May 1, 1835, Moore to Livingston, May 21, 1832, Mosquera to McAfee, July 12, 1833, Blackford to Webster, April 21, 1843, in Manning, V, 342, 465, 481, 593.

[5] May 26, 1837. See *Anales diplomáticos de Colombia*, III, 839.

[6] Rivas, *Relaciones*, p. 83.

[7] *Ibid.*, p. 92. For Semple's correspondence with the Department of State, see Manning, V, 559-589.

[8] *Anales diplomáticos de Colombia*, III, 164-165.

[9] It was submitted by Tyler on February 21, 1845. *Messages and Papers of the Presidents*, James D. Richardson, ed., IV, 364.

[10] Blackford to Pombo (extract), April 5, 1843, in Mendoza, p. 121.

[11] Richardson, *Messages and Papers*, IV, 511.

[12] Bidlack to Buchanan, December 14, 1846, same to same, May 14, 1847, Manning, V, 636, 649. The instructions were dated January 2, 1847, *ibid.*, p. 358.

[13] *Diary*, II, 363.

[14] Bidlack to Buchanan, December 9 and 10, 1846, Manning, V, 628, 633.

[15] *Ibid.*, p. 628.

[16] The best account of the Mosquito question from the New Granadan point of view is found in a series of articles written by Pedro Fernández Madrid and published in *El Día* of Bogotá from June to November, 1846, under the general title of "Nuestras Costas Incultas." The Library of Congress possesses a volume of *El Día* embracing these articles. Recently they have been reproduced by Raimundo Rivas in Volume I of *Escritos de don Pedro Fernández Madrid*. Fernández Madrid was for many years an underofficial in the department of foreign relations at Bogotá.

[17] Walter Cope (British Consul General at Quito) to Palmerston, November 7, 1846, Foreign Office, 97/156; Jewett to Buchanan, December 10, 1846, Department of State, Despatches from Peru, Vol. VII.

[18] As early as 1816 Lord Castlereagh warned J. Q. Adams that England might act *defensively* if the United States encroached upon its neighbors. See Adams, *Writings*, V, 502; also Rivas, *Escritos*, I, 273.

[19] Lorenzo Montúfar, *Reseña histórica de Centro América* (7 vols.; Guatemala, 1878-1888), IV, 93 ff.; Macdonald to Chief of the State of Nicaragua, August 15, 1841, and Aberdeen to Chatfield, April 13, 1842, F. O., 15/25, 29.

[20] "Nuestras Costas Incultas," in Rivas, *Escritos*, I, 231-233.

[21] In 1844 Patrick Walker was sent to Bluefields, capital of the mock kingdom, and as British agent and consul general he ruled the country during the next few years. His instructions and early correspondence are found in F. O., 53/1.

[22] The basis of the New Granadan claim was the royal order of San Lorenzo of November 30, 1803, by the terms of which, the government at Bogotá contended, the territory in question was definitely attached to the viceroyalty of New Granada. See "Nuestras Costas Incultas," in Rivas, *Escritos*, I, 248. The British held (Chatfield to Palmerston, January 30, 1847, F. O., 15/46) that the order was for military purposes only and could not make a political and jurisdictional change in the administration of the country.

[23] Rivas, *Escritos*, I, 183, 298.

[24] Pedro Dávalos y Lissón, *La primera centuria* (4 vols.; Lima, 1919-1926), IV, 77; printed statement signed "Equatoriano" received at the Foreign Office in December, 1846, F. O., 97/156; Rivas, *Escritos*, I, 303; London *Times*, November 28, 1846; Report (unsigned), November 3, 1846, F. O., 97/156.

[25] Memorial of the Committee of the South American and Mexican Association, in F. O., 97/156; Report, November 3, 1846, *ibid.*
[26] These memorials are all found in F. O., 97/156.
[27] H. U. Addison to Home Office, October 26, 1846, and Cope to Palmerston, November 7, 1846, *ibid.*
[28] H. U. Addison to J. D. Powles, October 26, 1846, *ibid.*
[29] F. O., 97/156.
[30] Flores to Palmerston, December [January ?] 9, 1847, F. O., 97/156. A fair account of the seizures was published in the London *Times* for November 28, 1846.
[31] Manning, V, 629–630.
[32] Flores to Palmerston, September [ ], 1846, and Palmerston to Flores, October 3, 1846, F. O., 97/156.
[33] January 9, 14, May 16, 1847, *ibid.*
[34] Flores to Palmerston, October 13, 1848, F. O., 21/1.
[35] Calvo to Wright, October 15, 1848, Secretaría de Relaciones Exteriores, Costa Rica. See also, in F. O., 53/11, a copy of a paper dated October 15, 1848, and entitled "Mis Opiniones." The name attached to the document is that of J. M. Flores, but that must have been an error of the copyist. The paper sets forth in detail a plan for the protectorate and is clearly the work of J. J. Flores.
[36] Flores to Palmerston, October 13, 1848, and Wright to Palmerston, F. O., 21/1.
[37] Flores to Palmerston, December 15, 1849, F. O., 21/2.
[38] Chatfield to Palmerston, March 8, 1850, and same to same, March 25, 1851, F. O., 15/64, 70.
[39] A congress of American states held at Lima in 1847 had as one of its objects the prevention of such undertakings as that contemplated by Flores. The war between the United States and Mexico was at the same time a matter of less concern. On this subject see, particularly, J. M. Torres Caicedo, *Unión Latino-Americana* (Paris, 1865), pp. 25, 45; Manning, V, 641–646; and J. Randolph Clay to Buchanan, January 12, 1848, Department of State, Despatches from Peru, Vol. VII.

TOLEDO'S FLORIDA INTRIGUES

[1] The Pan-American bearing of this paper does not appear on the surface. The reader will perceive, however, that if Toledo had succeeded in carrying out his plans the entire history of the New World would have been profoundly affected.
[2] I. J. Cox, "Monroe and the Early Mexican Revolutionary Agents," *Annual Report of the American Historical Association, 1911,* I, 203.
[3] Vincente Pazos, *The Exposition, Remonstrance and Protest of Don Vincente Pazos, Commissioner on behalf of the Republican Agents established on Amelia Island, in Florida, under the authority and in behalf of the Independent States of South America. . . .* Presented to the Executive of the United States on the ninth of February, 1818. Translated from the Spanish. Philadelphia, 1818.
[4] Carlos M. Trelles, "Un Precursor de la Independencia de Cuba: Don José Alvarez de Toledo," *Discursos leídos en la recepción pública del Sr. Carlos M. Trelles y Govín* (Havana, 1926), pp. 49, 77, 84.
[5] "Manifiesto ó Satisfacción Pundomorosa, á Todos los Españoles Europeos, y á Todos los Pueblos de la América, por un Diputado de las Cortes Reunidas en Cádiz," in Trelles, *Discursos,* Appendix II.

Notes

[6] Wellesley to Castlereagh, July 6, 1819 (Private and Confidential), Foreign Office, 72/225.

[7] Onis to Bardaxi y Arara, September 25 and December 28, 1811, Archivo Histórico Nacional, Estado, Legajo 5554; same to same, January 20, 1812, A. H. N., Est., Leg. 5638.

[8] Juan Mariano Picornell and Father Sedella were able to join the torn pieces of the commission together and make a copy which Sedella sent to Onis under date of July 9, 1816. Cf. Onis to Cevallos, August 11, 1816, A. H. N., Est., Leg. 5554. Another copy was intercepted by royalist forces in Mexico in 1815. Cf. Trelles, *Discursos*, p. 153.

[9] Communication was carried on for the most part through A. J. Dallas as an intermediary. See Dallas to Monroe, November 25, December 4, and December 25, 1811, Department of State, Miscellaneous Letters.

[10] Onis to Pezuela, October 7, 1812, A. H. N., Est., Leg. 5554. Under date of January 7, 1812, Toledo wrote Monroe in veiled terms about setting out on his mission. State Dept., Misc.

[11] The name was generally shortened, contemporaneously, to Bernardo, rather than to Gutiérrez, or to Lara.

[12] "Diary of José Bernardo Gutiérrez de Lara," *American Historical Review*, XXXIV, 71–77.

[13] Dallas to Graham, January 4, 1812, State Dept., Misc. Toledo also received divers sums from William Shaler in Louisiana. See Shaler to Monroe, May 16, 1813, State Dept., Spec. Agts.

[14] "Diary of José Bernardo Gutiérrez de Lara," *American Historical Review*, XXXIV, 286–294; Claiborne to Shaler, April 7, 1812, State Dept., Spec. Agts.

[15] Shaler to Monroe, May 2, May 7, June 12, June 23, August 18, August 25, 1812, State Dept., Spec. Agts.

[16] *Discursos*, 23, 27.

[17] Shaler to Monroe, November 13, November 25, December 6, December 8, December 27, 1811, State Dept., Spec. Agts. The letter of November 25, an endorsement shows, was received at the State Department on December 17. (The writer is indebted to Mr. Hunter Miller, Historical Adviser of the State Department, for this information.) An earlier letter of Shaler's required only twelve days to reach Washington. It is not unlikely, therefore, that Monroe had received Shaler's letter of December 8 by the end of that month.

[18] Cogswell to Gutiérrez and Magee, December 29, 1812 [Extract], State Dept., Spec. Agts. See also in this connection Shaler to Gutiérrez, May 28, 1813, and Shaler to Monroe, June 12, 1813, State Dept., Spec. Agts.

[19] Miranda had recently surrendered to the royalist forces in Venezuela. The belief was common that he had played the part of traitor. That view is no longer held.

[20] The Marquis of Villafranca was in effect a member of the Cortes, and the Duke of Infantado had been a member of the Regency since January 21, 1812. Lafuente, *Historia general de España*, XVII, 269, 460. Toledo may have been related to the Duke of Infantado (Pedro Alcántara de Toledo) as well as to the Marquis of Villafranca. Cf. Trelles, *Discursos*, 44–45.

[21] The letter was sent to the postmaster at Natchitoches, who consulted Shaler before sending the packet on by express. There is a possibility that Shaler may have acquainted himself with the contents of the letter before it was allowed to proceed. See Jno. Johnston [postmaster at Pittsburgh] to the postmaster at Nat-

chitoches, December 29, 1813, and Shaler to Monroe, February 26, 1813, State Dept., Spec. Agts.

[22] Shaler to Monroe, April 18, 1813, State Dept., Spec. Agts.; Morphy to the Viceroy of New Spain, May 8 and 25, 1813, Archivo General, Mexico, Guerra, Notas Diplomáticas, III.

[23] Shaler to Monroe, February 26, 1813, State Dept., Spec. Agts.

[24] Shaler to Monroe, May 7, 1813, State Dept., Spec. Agts.; Morphy to the Viceroy of New Spain, May 21, 1813, A. G. M., Guerra, N. D., III.

[25] Toledo to Monroe, May 6, 1813, State Dept., Spec. Agts.

[26] Shaler to Monroe, May 7, 1813, H. A. Bullard to Shaler, June 27, 1813, Jas. B. Wilkinson to Shaler, June 27, 1813, State Dept., Spec. Agts.

[27] Shaler to Monroe, September 5 and September 19, 1813, State Dept., Spec. Agts.; Onis to Labrador, October 8, 1813, A. H. N., Est., Leg. 5639.

[28] Arredondo to the Junta de Guerra, April 10, 1817, A. G. M., Historia, Tomo 152.

[29] Alamán, *Historia de Méjico*, III, 488; Zamacois, *Historia de Méjico*, IX, 216; Bancroft, *North Mexican States and Texas*, II, 31; Yoakum, *History of Texas*, I, 173–175; Trelles, *op. cit.*

[30] Onis to Pezuela, A. H. N., Est., Leg. 5554.

[31] So stated by Onis in a later letter [to Ferdinand VII] dated September 19, 1819. A. H. N., Est., Leg. 5554.

[32] Onis to Pezuela, October 7, 1812, A. H. N., Est., Leg. 5554.

[33] Onis to Labrador, March 4, 1813, A. H. N., Est., Leg. 5554.

[34] Onis to Labrador, August 18, 1813, A. H. N., Est., Leg. 5639.

[35] Onis to Labrador, October 8, 1813, A. H. N., Est., Leg. 5639.

[36] Trelles, *Discursos*, 131.

[37] *American State Papers, Foreign Relations*, IV, 431.

[38] Trelles, *Discursos*, 33.

[39] Onis to the Viceroy of New Spain, October 26, 1815, and numerous other documents in A. G. M., Guerra, N. D., III, bear on this subject.

[40] This is an example: "Por una carta qe acabo de recibir del Vice-Consul Ynterino de S. M. de Nueva Orleans Don Diego Morphy, aparece qe la Goleta Petit Milan, qe Toledo habia enviado a Boquilla de Piedra, con cantidad de armas, municiones, proclamas, y otros efectos, ha perecido con todo su cargamento."—Onis to Cevallos, March 30, 1816, A. H. N., Est., Leg. 5641.

[41] Cogswell to Gutiérrez and Magee, December 29, 1812 [Extract], State Dept., Spec. Agts.

[42] *Toledo lo manda siempre por delante.*—Morphy to the Viceroy of New Spain, June 11, 1813, A. G. M., Guerra, N. D., III.

[43] Trelles, *Discursos*, 139; Apodaca to O'Donojú, March 30, 1814, Archivo General de Indias, Papeles de Cuba, Leg. 1856.

[44] Onis to the Viceroy of New Spain, January 8, 1816, and other letters in A. G. M., Guerra, N. D., III.

[45] See an undated report of Onis in A. H. N., Est., Leg. 5554 (L. C., p. 1126).

[46] Onis to Cevallos, August 11, 1816, A. H. N., Est., Leg. 5554.

[47] Onis to Cevallos, July 7, 1816, A. H. N., Est., Leg. 5641, and the letter cited in note 46. Toledo's formal application for pardon was dated at Philadelphia, December 12, 1816. The document is in A. H. N., Est., Leg. 5554. Trelles, basing his narrative on the *Memorias* of García de León Pizarro, gives the date of this communication as December 12, 1815. This is manifestly an error.

[48] Onis to Cevallos, August 30, 1816, A. H. N., Est., Leg. 5554. For the develop-

Notes

ment of this intrigue see Onis to Cevallos, September 16, 1816, A. H. N., Est., Leg. 5641, and same to same in Leg. 5554 under dates of October 20, 1816, November 16, 1816, and November 23, 1816.

[49] Letter cited above under date of August 30, 1816. The discussion between Toledo and Mina on the subject of Florida is inferred.

[50] Graham to Monroe, September 12, 1816, Monroe Papers, New York Public Library.

[51] Pazos was connected with the Amelia Island establishment at the time of its suppression in December, 1817. See note 2.

[52] Onis to Monroe, July 22, August 28, August 29, and September 11, 1816 (the last with affidavits enclosed), State Dept., Notes from the Spanish Legation; Monroe to Onis, August 16 and September 12, 1816, State Dept., Foreign Legations, Notes.

[53] William Davis Robinson, *Memoirs of the Mexican Revolution, Including a Narrative of the Expedition of General Xavier Mina* (Philadelphia, 1820), p. 57.

[54] Robinson, *op. cit.*; Simón Bolívar to Maxwell Hyslop, September 26, and October 4, 1816, in *Cartas del Libertador* (Lecuna ed.), I, 252–253.

[55] September 17, 1816, in O'Leary, *Memorias*, XI, 348. This letter was obviously misdated, for Mina did not arrive at Port au Prince until early in October. Cf. Robinson, *Memoirs*, p. 57, and the letters of Bolívar cited in note 54.

[56] *Memoirs*, p. 76. Charles Morris, commanding the United States frigate *Congress*, reported the rumored attack by Mina in a letter to the secretary of the navy under date of March 14, 1817. See extract of his letter in State Dept., Despatches from Consuls. The British consul at New Orleans gave similar information under date of March 4, 1817, F. O., 115/27.

[57] Robinson, *Memoirs*, p. 261.

[58] The correspondence relating to the expedition is found in A. G. M., Historia, Tomo 152.

[59] Onis to Cevallos, August 30, 1816, A. H. N., Est., Leg. 5554.

[60] Onis to Cevallos, September 11, 1816, A. H. N., Est., Leg. 5641.

[61] Onis to Cevallos, December 7, 1816, A. H. N., Est., Leg. 5641. Robinson gives a circumstantial account (*Memoirs*, pp. 69–71) of a mutiny at Galveston Island led by a certain Correa, who was an agent of Onis. The plot was discovered and Onis's part in it exposed. In writing to his government (December 7, 1816, A. H. N., Est., Leg. 5641), Onis mentioned the charge but did not deny it.

[62] *Niles' Weekly Register*, XI, 64 (September 21, 1816); *ibid.*, XI, 106 (October 12, 1816); *ibid.*, XII, 46 (March 15, 1817). See also Captain Charles Morris to the secretary of the navy [Extracts], March 14, and April 17, 1817, State Dept., Despatches from Consuls.

[63] From 1808 to 1814 there were two governments in Spain: one at Madrid under French auspices, and another at Cádiz under a regency in the name of the captive Ferdinand. Onis came to the United States in 1809 as the representative of the government at Cádiz; but he was not received until 1815. The government at Madrid was not recognized.

[64] Onis to Cevallos, May 30, 1816, A. H. N., Est., Leg. 5660.

[65] Adams to Monroe, March 30, 1816, Manning, *Diplomatic Correspondence*, III, 1437; Erving to Monroe (Private and Confidential), September 22, 1816, Monroe Papers, N. Y. Pub. Lib.

[66] Onis to Cevallos, August 11, 1816, A. H. N., Est., Leg. 5554.

[67] Onis to Cevallos, August 30, 1816, A. H. N., Est., Leg. 5554.
[68] Onis to Cevallos, August 11, 1816, A. H. N., Est., Leg. 5554.
[69] Onis to Cevallos, August 30, 1816, A. H. N., Est., Leg. 5554.
[70] August 21, 1816, State Dept., Misc.
[71] Letter to Monroe, September 3, 1816, State Dept., Misc.
[72] Jesup to Monroe, August 21, 1816, State Dept., Misc.; Jesup to Claiborne, August 24, 1816, Claiborne Papers, Library of Congress.
[73] Madison to Monroe, September 22, 1816, Monroe Papers, N. Y. Pub. Lib.
[74] J. Q. Adams to John Adams, August 1, 1816, J. Q. Adams, *Writings*, VI, 61.
[75] C. K. Webster, *The Foreign Policy of Castlereagh* (London, 1925), 408, 437.
[76] On January 1, 1816, Onis reported to Cevallos that the news from England regarding the supposed cession had caused general consternation, that General Jackson, then in Washington, was holding frequent conferences with the President, and that nobody doubted that Jackson was going to be given command of an army to take possession of the Floridas. A. H. N., Est., Leg. 5641.
[77] Adams to Monroe, February 8, 1816, *Writings*, V, 502.
[78] Rush, *Memoranda of a Residence at the Court of London* (ed. of 1833), p. 488.
[79] *Messages and Papers of the Presidents*, J. D. Richardson, ed., II, 24.
[80] Monroe to [Graham], September 17, 1816, State Dept., Misc.
[81] January 10, 1817, F. O., 72/196.
[82] See T. Frederick Davis, "MacGregor's Invasion of Florida, 1817," *Florida Historical Society Quarterly*, July, 1928.
[83] The captain general of Cuba to the minister of war, June 12, 1816, Trelles, *Discursos*, p. 97.
[84] Onis to Cevallos, November 23, December 4, 1816, A. H. N., Est., Leg. 5554; same to same, December 7, 1816, A. H. N., Est., Leg. 5641; Onis to captain general of Cuba, December 8, 1816, A. G. I., Papeles de Cuba, Leg. 1898.
[85] *Baltimore Patriot and Evening Advertizer*. The letters were published in the issues of December 2 and December 4, 1816.
[86] Onis to Cevallos, December 7, 1816, A. H. N., Est., Leg. 5641.
[87] Trelles, *Discursos*, pp. 40–42.
[88] Wellesley to Castlereagh (Private and Confidential), July 6, 1819, F. O., 72/225.
[89] Castlereagh to Wellesley (Private and Confidential), July 21, 1819, F. O., 72/222.

Notes

SHALER'S PAN-AMERICAN SCHEME

[1] Though William Shaler never achieved great fame, he was a man of more than ordinary attainments. After a varied experience as the captain of a vessel engaged in the fur trade on the northwest coast of America, he entered the public service of the United States. He received his first appointment, as a special agent to Mexico, in 1810. The slow progress of the revolution led him in 1813 to abandon the mission and return to Washington. Two years later he was designated as a commissioner to Algiers. The treaty which he signed there under the guns of Decatur's squadron brought the hostilities between the United States and that country to an end. He remained at Algiers as consul general until 1829, when he was transferred in a like capacity to Havana, Cuba. There he died in 1833, at the age of fifty-five. Shaler published in 1808, in the *American Register* (III, 136-175), a "Journal of a Voyage from China to the Northwestern Coast of America in 1804," which contains what is believed to be the first description of California by an American writer. He published also, as by-products of his residence in Algiers, a paper on the "Language of the Berbers in Africa," which appeared in the *American Philosophical Transactions*, and a book entitled *Sketches of Algiers*. See *Appleton's Cyclopedia of American Biography; North American Review*, XXII, 409-431; Malloy, *Treaties*, I; Adelaide R. Haase, *Index to United States Documents Relating to Foreign Affairs*, III; R. G. Cleland, *A History of California: The American Period*, pp. 13-16, 471-482; *Niles' Weekly Register*, XLIV, 113; "A Narrative of Voyages and Commercial Enterprises" in *Voyages and Travels* (Edward Moxon, London, 1850). Thanks are due to Dr. R. G. Cleland for this last reference.

[2] J. B. Lockey, *Pan-Americanism: Its Beginnings* (New York, 1920), p. 288.

[3] From a photostatic reproduction lent by the Florida State Historical Society. The original is in the State Department, Special Agents, Shaler to Monroe, August 18, 1812.

BOLIVAR AFTER A CENTURY

[1] See *National Intelligencer*, February 14, 1831; New York *Daily Advertiser*, February 15, 1831; *Niles' Register*, February 19, 1831; London *Times*, February 19, 1831; *Journal des Débats*, February 21, 1831.

[2] This account, which was published on February 21, 1831, and translations of the accounts of other Paris newspapers of the same date, are found in *Documentos para la historia de la vida pública del Libertador*, José Félix Blanco and Ramón Azpurúa, comps. (14 vols.; Caracas, 1875-1877), XIV, 515-522.

[3] Among De Pradt's works are the following: *Des Colonies et de la Révolution Actuelle de l'Amérique* (2 vols.; Paris, 1817), *L'Europe et l'Amérique, depuis le Congrès d'Aix-la-Chapelle* (2 vols.; Paris, 1821-1822), *L'Europe et l'Amérique en 1821* (2 vols.; Paris, 1822), *L'Europe et l'Amérique en 1822 et 1823* (2 vols.; Paris, 1824), *Congrès de Panama* (Paris, 1825), *Concordat de l'Amérique avec Rome* (Paris, 1827).

[4] Bolívar to De Pradt, November 15, 1824, *Cartas del Libertador*, Vicente Lecuna, ed. (10 vols.; Caracas, 1929), IV, 209.

[5] Felipe Larrazabal, *Vida del Libertador, Simón Bolívar*, R. Blanco-Fombona, ed. (2 vols.; Madrid, 1918), I, 245-248.

[6] Bolívar to Maxwell Hyslop, May 19, 1815, *Cartas del Libertador,* I, 148.
[7] May 21, 1823, *Cartas del Libertador,* III, 188.
[8] Published under the title, *Simón Bolívar—Un pensamiento sobre el Congreso de Panamá, Obsequio de Vicente Lecuna a los delegados al Segundo Congreso Científico Pan-Americano* (Washington, 1916).
[9] How different now, less than a decade since this paper was written!

PAN-AMERICANISM AND IMPERIALISM

[1] Whatever the appearance to the contrary, the peoples of the New World are attached to the democratic ideal. Governments come and go, but the ideal remains as the unifying principle.
[2] For an interesting discussion of this subject, see an article by E. G. Bourne in the *Annual Report of the American Historical Association for 1899,* pp. 155–169.
[3] See speech delivered in the Senate on December 21, 1870, *Complete Works,* XVIII, 292.
[4] By a treaty signed at Washington, May 29, 1934. See *American Journal of International Law,* Suppl., Vol. XXVIII (1934), p. 97.
[5] *U. S. Statutes at Large,* XLVIII, 456.

ST. MARY'S COLLEGE OF MARYLAND
ST. MARY'S CITY, MARYLAND

C57971